CHRISTY JOHNSON

Love Junkies

7 STEPS FOR BREAKING THE
TOXIC RELATIONSHIP CYCLE

CHRISTY
JOHNSON.ORG

Love Junkies
Copyright © 2014 by Christy Johnson
Copyright © 2018 by Christy Johnson 2nd printing

Cover design by Rob Williams, InsideOut Design
Edited by Keith Wall

Unless otherwise specified, Scripture quotations are taken from *The Holy Bible, New International Version*® NIV®. Copyright © 1973, 1978, 1984, 2011 by Biblica, Inc.™ Used by permission of Zondervan. All rights reserved worldwide. www.zondervan.com. The "NIV" and "New International Version" are trademarks registered in the United States Patent and Trademark Office by Biblica, Inc.™

Other versions used are:

AMP—Scripture quotations taken from the *Amplified*® *Bible*, Copyright © 1954, 1958, 1962, 1964, 1965, 1987 by The Lockman Foundation. Used by permission. (www.Lockman.org).

KJV—*King James Version,* Authorized King James Version.

NASB—Scripture taken from the *New American Standard Bible*®, Copyright © 1960, 1962, 1963, 1968, 1971, 1972, 1973, 1975, 1977, 1995 by The Lockman Foundation. Used by permission. (www.Lockman.org).

NKJV—Scripture taken from the *New King James Version.* Copyright © 1982 by Thomas Nelson, Inc. Used by permission. All rights reserved.

NLT—Scripture quotations marked (NLT) are taken from the *Holy Bible, New Living Translation,* copyright © 1996, 2004, 2007 by Tyndale House Foundation. Used by permission of Tyndale House Publishers, Inc., Carol Stream, Illinois 60188. All rights reserved.

Published by Christy Johnson
Edmond, OK 73013

Library of Congress Cataloging-in-Publication Data

Johnson, Christy

　　Love Junkies: 7 steps for breaking the toxic relationship cycle / Christy Johnson
p. cm.

ISBN 978-1-7320193-0-0

　　978-1-7320193-1-7 (e-book)

Printed in the United States of America

21 20 19 18 17 16 15 14   10 9 8 7 6 5 4 3 2 1

I dedicate this book to
my husband, John.

Since the day you proposed and
ever since we've been married,
you've always said that your purpose in life
is to see my purpose fulfilled.
I'm in awe of that sacrifice.
Thank you for being a rock of security for me.
It's because of your support and
encouragement that this book is a reality.

foreword

Where's the book for ME?

Between 1996 and 1998, this thought thrashed around in my mind with each bookstore we entered. Both my husband and I meticulously combed the shelves for a book that would deliver the tidal wave of hope and comfort I needed. There were plenty of books for the male sex addict ... or for the wife of the male sex addict ... but nothing for *me*. I'd come to identify myself as a *female love addict*, in desperate need of recovery, a man-junkie who'd been strung out on more relationships than I cared to count.

In 2001, I was blessed to sign a contract to write the very book I'd searched for but never found. When I crafted *Every Woman's Battle* (as a companion book to *Every Man's Battle* by Stephen Arterburn, Fred Stoeker, and Mike Yorkey), my prayer was never that it become *the* book for women, but rather *one of many* books for women struggling to overcome dysfunctional patterns of trying to spell love M-A-N rather than G-O-D.

I frequently prayed that the Holy Spirit would use *Every Woman's Battle* to raise up many other disciples for the messages of sexual integrity, sexual intimacy only within marriage, and spiritual intimacy with Jesus Christ, the Ultimate Lover we've all longed for. There needed to be an entire army of women on a re-con mission to recover the many sisters who've gotten lost in their own reckless pursuits of romantic intoxication.

That's why, a decade later, I was delighted to meet Christy Johnson when she applied to participate in my online mentorship program, BLAST (Building Leaders, Authors, Speakers, & Teachers). As I learned about her heart to reach love-starved women with a message of freedom and deliverance ... as I watched snippets of her powerful testimony at christyjohnson.org ... as I witnessed her masterfully win the hearts of her audience with every video submitted and every live presentation she made ... I knew that Christy Johnson was a BIG answer to my previous prayers.

When Christy shared with me the manuscript you're now holding, I knew this message *had* to be published so that other women could get their hands on it as well. With clarity and confidence, with boldness and brilliance, with sensitivity and sincerity, Christy offers the very tidal wave of hope and healing that I was in search of almost two decades ago.

So today is your lucky day if you're one of the millions of women on the planet who have asked, "When will I be loved? Why can't I find the right guy? Where's the book for *me*?" You just found the answers to these very questions.

Shannon Ethridge
www.shannonethridge.com
www.blastmentoring.com

Acknowledgments

I FIRST WANT TO THANK the women who taught and mentored me when my life was a wreck. Without your listening ears, compassionate hugs, and sometimes very-needed stern wisdom and direction, I wouldn't be who I am today. Because of your guidance, I know the powerful transformation that takes place when women submit to discipleship. Christy Baker, Elizabeth Dungan, and Melissa Thompson, you'll never know the power of the words you spoke over me when my life was a love-junkie mess. I believe God hand-picked each of you to develop me in the darkroom of my life. You saw the finished picture when I was still a wet-sloppy negative. Thank you from the bottom of my heart.

To my ministry mentor, Shannon Ethridge. Wow, what can I say? I'm astounded at God's plans to make our paths cross, but how you poured yourself into me is beyond amazing. Thank you for your investment in the next generation of writers and speakers through your BLAST (Building Leaders Authors Speakers and Teachers) program. I'm forever grateful for your encouragement, support, and friendship.

Mo Anderson, vice chair of Keller Williams, I'm astounded that the very first time we met, you pulled out your checkbook and generously gave seed money to birth my dream. I know you have a heart to see women set free from the trappings of toxic relationships. May you see a hundred-fold return on your gift.

Pastor Mark Crow, Barb Swanson, Cynthia Huffmyer, Masie Bross, Bea Jai Webb, and Bishop Tony Miller, you are incredible thought leaders with contagious visions. Your passionate leadership has taught me how to lead my own army of women. Thank you!

Julie Gorman, thank you for initiating contact with a total stranger and taking the time to connect me to the Authentic team, who captured the vision for this book. You are a gem!

Kyle Duncan, thank you for taking a chance on a first-time author. You are truly a Sherpa, my personal guide taking me up the publishing mountain. I'm eternally grateful for your direction. You make it possible for me to lead other women out of the wilderness of relationship addiction.

Tina Strickling, what an amazing woman and friend you are. You don't see flaws. You don't see failure. You only see futures. Thank you for teaching me how to increase my vision and how to value myself. With my old belief system, this manuscript would have never made it past my own desk.

To my dear friends Dru Atkinson, Darla Muralt, Jenny Broughton, and many others too numerous to mention here, thank you for your friendship and countless hours of listening to me talk about my "project." To all my writer buddies, you are the real cheerleaders! Your prayers and encouragement gave me courage to keep going, despite the constant rejections writers live with.

To all the women who told me their stories that are sprinkled throughout this book; thank you for sharing your relationship struggles. Your tears and triumphs will be instrumental in helping others receive their own hope and healing.

John, my darling husband, I could not have done this without you. I'm sure you had no idea of the road ahead when you asked me to marry you, but through all the highs and lows, you've supported my vision both financially and emotionally. God knew what He was doing when He picked you out for me.

Speaking of God, I want to thank Him most of all. There was a day when I was afraid to give my heart to God because I thought He'd send me off to Africa. (Isn't that where all Christians go?) Little did I know how much I would enjoy the perfect mission He had planned for me—empowering women to live soul-healthy lives.

And last but not at all least, I want to thank my children, Brittany, Melissa and Garrett. Even though you are now adults living on your own, the call to write came while you were still at home. You never complained when I was busy writing. Maybe you wished I was a normal mom, whatever that is. Instead you embraced my vision and cheered me on, even when it meant many sacrifices on your part. I love you each so much. I know that your patience with my calling is a seed planted into your own destiny. It's thrilling to see God develop each of you!

And for Jakey Poo (Jake), my two-and-a-half-year-old son who preceded me into heaven . . . it was your death that gave me a glimpse of my own destiny. I believe you passed me your baton and are cheering me on from heaven to finish my race. I can't wait to see you on the other side.

Contents

−1−

When Men Are a Drug

"YOU'RE HAVING AN AFFAIR, aren't you?" my husband demanded as he slammed the door to our two-bedroom apartment in Kansas City. He pounded his clenched fist against the wall. The oriental print hanging above the entry table swung back and forth a few times before it stopped off-center.

Panic whipped through my stomach.

"Aren't you?" he yelled, louder this time. His face was rage-red.

I froze, not even looking up from my newspaper.

Tom grabbed the paper and threw it aside on the couch.

"I've been wondering why you've been out of town so much," he spat.

"Whatever," I replied, scowling as I jerked away from his domination. "And what are you doing at home? You're supposed to be out looking for a job."

Tom bent over to get eye level with me. His breath reeked with a familiar chemical smell and his speech was slurred. I could tell he had been using drugs again.

"Get out of my face," I said. "You're messed up again."

"Now it all makes sense," he hissed, moving closer. "There's someone at work, isn't there?"

I shook my head. "If you weren't so messed up all the time, maybe we could have a decent conversation."

"You can deny it all you want, but I asked Pastor Dan."

I stood up and looked straight in his face. "Oh, right," I said, laser-locking my eyes with his. *Pastor Dan wouldn't betray me. He promised that our counseling sessions were confidential.* "You're lying! He didn't tell you that."

"Actually, he didn't say a word. But if it weren't true, he would have defended you. Just admit it!"

Tom ripped his coat off and flung it on the wicker chair. The metal zipper grazed my arm before it landed.

"Watch what you're doing!" I picked up the newspaper that had been strewn all over the couch. "If this marriage—if that's what you even want to call it—has a problem, it's not an affair. It's all your empty promises and lies."

Trying to avoid his unrelenting glare, I picked up a few scattered toys on the floor and put them in the basket by the television.

Tom crouched down and locked eyes with me. "You're cheating, aren't you?"

Chilled blood pumped through my veins. There was no escape.

He *knew.*

I gazed at the beige carpet. A purple stain begged to be blotted. "If you weren't such a lousy husband, I wouldn't have needed anyone else," I sobbed. "The past-due bills. Your drug addiction. It's too much. I can't take it anymore."

BUSTED AND DISGUSTED

Throughout our marriage, issues in our relationship strangled me. Because of my own brokenness, however, I thought all the problems were my husband's fault. After years of futile attempts to change him, I had given up. Instead of the happily-ever-after I'd dreamed of, I settled for pain relief in the arms of another man. Even though Tom and I were going to marriage counseling, I was oblivious to my own invisible prison of bitterness. I thought my happiness was tied to my husband—if only he would change, I could be happy.

I had yet to learn that broken people attract broken people, and broken people hurt each other. Until the brokenness is fixed, an invisible vacuum sucks us into a merry-go-round of chaos sprinkled with just enough temporary peace that momentarily deceives us into thinking that everything is going to work out after all.

In a way I found relief that day. My secret was out. Even though I had nowhere else to run, at least I no longer had to hide behind my lies.

My problems started long before I met Tom. In high school, I spent every Friday night glued to the television. Truly, everything I learned about romance I learned from *The Love Boat*. By the time I figured out that real devotion comes from a friendship, not a cruise ship, it was too late—I was already hooked. Turns out I got old too soon and smart too late.

By the time Tom and I were engaged, I had made him responsible for my emotional welfare. My heart was in his hands,

> *I thought my happiness was tied to my husband—if only he would change, I could be happy.*

and like a sports fan on Super Bowl Sunday, he controlled the remote. His actions dictated whether or not I was happy. He controlled whether or not I was depressed. His behavior influenced my sense of peace. I gave him the lockbox of my heart and threw away the key. At one time, I thought this sounded romantic.

Not now.

I'm not alone. Countless women everywhere are hurting in the hands of love, misguided by romantic notions based on fantasies and fairy tales. Emily tends to rush into relationships, believing what men tell her instead of taking the time to watch their actions. After her divorce from Ron, who had a gambling addiction, she rushed into a relationship with Michael, who was a workaholic. He was responsible with money, but she never saw him.

Cheryl is naïve. She falls for smooth talkers and phony profiles. Two men she dated recently turned out to be married.

Erin puts her own needs in her marriage last. Even though she's tried to change, she always puts her husband's needs first, not out of respect but out of her own insecurities. She is constantly compromising, even though it makes her angry.

Keisha struggles with infidelity in her marriage. For her, it's easier to have an affair, even if it's an emotional affair, than to expect improvement in her marriage.

I've had my own share of affairs, both physical and emotional. I'm a happily married woman today, but I wasn't always so lucky in love. Like the woman at the well encountered by Jesus, I was a big-time loser when it came to relationships. I was a love junkie, and men were my drug of choice.

Some women are born with the ability to choose men wisely and have successful relationships. Not me. My picker was busted. For starters, I was so naïve that I couldn't distinguish the guy from the lie. And because I was so needy (that sounds better than desperate), I looked for acceptance, worth, validation, and approval in my relationships with men. Since I had no real identity of my own, I saw no other choice. Besides, relationships were a clever cover-up—the perfect disguise for my addiction.

Until I had my own encounter with Jesus, which changed my life.

Oh, I had met Jesus before. I gave Him my heart at summer camp in high school. My relationship with Christ was very important to me, but even after I accepted His gift of salvation my insecurities caused me to discount His love for me. Deep inside, I doubted I deserved the type of love I longed for. I struggled to believe I was worthy. My fears and inadequacies compelled me to seek false approval and camouflage my pain. On the outside, I looked happy and whole, but on the inside, I was desperate for love. So, over and over I ran from relationship to relationship to relationship. The counterfeit approval I found from men always left me wanting more, but it was better than nothing.

Three years into my first marriage, my husband and I separated. I was afraid and alone. I didn't know how to be alone. In the past I dealt with my loneliness by looking for love. The anticipation of a new relationship masked the pain. But now, I was in a different place emotionally and spiritually. After affairs in my marriage nearly destroyed my life, I was committed to dealing with my demons and the bondage that my addiction to relationships previously held me in.

I sat in my living room one afternoon. My fingers tingled as I rubbed them against the fabric of my couch. *Why am I like this?* I wondered. *Why have I always needed a man to feel complete?* I had never contemplated this question before. I had never allowed myself to be alone long enough to consider it. I wasn't expecting an answer, not from myself or anyone else, yet an answer came. It wasn't audible, but I knew it was from God.

"Because you've never believed you were worthy to receive what you really wanted, you settled for less in relationships."

Suddenly, the tingling in my fingers crept throughout my entire body. I sensed His presence in the room and I heard His voice: "To you, less was better than nothing. But because one relationship was never enough to fill the void, you always had another relationship on the side."

I glanced at the antique footstool beneath my feet. The finish was worn off on the corner, but to me, the distressed edges only added to its character. I heard—or sensed—God's words again: "Just like that footstool, Christy, I love you just the way you are. What you've perceived as flaws actually add to your beauty. I celebrate every part of you."

I felt God's love wrap around me and the weight of performance slither to the ground. All my life I had performed for others in order to gain their approval. No more! For the first time in my life, I was alone, but I didn't feel alone. In an instant, the revelation of how much Christ loved me and approved of me became so real that the thought of accepting anything less nauseated me. I became repulsed at the thought that I had used men for approval and affirmation. In that moment, God liberated me from the opinions of others, and I accepted His freedom to be the unique woman He created me to be.

I began my journey of recovery from relationship addiction that day. I was still married, but little by little, day by day, I laid down my need for approval from my husband and transferred it to Christ. It was a long journey. As liberating as the freedom was at times, there were also many days of pain and sorrow. I'd take two steps forward and one step back, but the net effect was always progress. I've never regretted the choice I made to surrender my trust to Christ and allow Him to restore my soul.

He wants to restore your soul, too. Will you let Him? That's what this book is all about—a healing journey of transforming liberty for love junkies. From one love junkie to another, I'll take you by the hand and show you how to navigate past the pain and move toward Jesus. This is not a book from someone who has no clue. I've lived in the pit and know what it's like. I've been distressed and now I'm blessed and because of that, my hope is overflowing for you. I'm convinced that if this love junkie found liberty, you can too.

THE LEAST LIKELY TO SUCCEED

I'm certain there are others more qualified to write this book, but I've noticed something about God: He often picks the least likely to succeed. At least this is true in my case.

A couple of months after I repented of my extramarital affairs and left the wilderness of my own relationship addiction, I had my first vision. I had never heard anyone talk about visions before, but I instinctively knew that what I saw was from God. When God reveals Himself to you, whether it's through a dream, a divine encounter, or a vision, you don't need an introduction—you just *know* it's Him.

Moses did. He took off his sandals.

The woman at the well did. She ran back to town to tell everyone.

Gideon did too. But not until after he questioned the Lord's angel. "Me? You want to use me? Are you sure you have the right guy? My clan is the weakest in Manasseh, and I am the least in my family."

> *If you surrender your life and your relationships to God, He will make you whole and complete and lacking no good thing.*

I felt like Gideon. God could not have chosen a more unlikely candidate for the job He was giving me.

I had barely begun my own journey of recovery. Why God chose to reveal this to me then, I'm not sure. He gave Joseph a dream, years before Joseph became second in command over Egypt. He anointed David when he was a teenager, years before David was appointed king. And like Gideon, He called me long before I was capable of the assignment to which He was calling me.

In my vision, I saw myself standing on top of a mountain in a desert. A single-file line of women were making a journey toward me. The line of women spiraled around the mountain numerous times and off into the desert as far as I could see.

I couldn't image what all the women were traveling to see and why I was on the top of the mountain. "Lord, what does this mean?" I asked.

"These are the women you will help."

"Me? Are you kidding? I've just barely begun to trust You, Lord! Plus, don't you remember speech class in junior high? I was the one who needed CPR after delivering my monologue."

"I will equip you. And you will help women come out of the wilderness of relationship addiction and take the journey to the top of the mountain, into My presence."

I didn't want to speak to women. I just wanted to be whole. I never could have imagined how God could use an invalid to influence others. But God is the restorer of our souls. He saw something in me long before I could, and He must have known—without a vision to press toward, I might succumb to the challenge of adversity and remain trapped in the wilderness, ordained by Satan to live a dry and bitter life.

God spoke to me before I fully experienced my freedom from relationship addiction. Interestingly, I wasn't a writer at the time, but the multitude of women God was telling me I would help were in a single-file line—like the women reading this book. *Love Junkies* may have been published for the masses, but as you read, I speak to each of you one by one.

God longs to speak to you too. He wants to bind your hurts and heal them. He wants to restore your soul from the bondage of relationship addiction. If you surrender your life and your relationships to Him, He will make you whole and complete and lacking no good thing.

As you read this book, my prayer is that Jesus will restore your soul—and that you will never encounter the dying thirst of an unhealthy relationship again. I've found that freedom in Christ, and I long for you to experience it too.

There would be no greater joy for me than to see my sisters take their own journeys out of the wilderness of relationship addiction and into the presence of God. May we all be like the woman at the well who encountered the hope of Christ. She ran to grab her sisters and bring them all to see the man who promised a life of freedom. And now, as I look out from the top of the mountain toward the horizon, I see that line of women forming.

Out of the wilderness—one by one, and into the presence of God.

So, come on, girlfriend! Won't you join me at the top of the mountain? God has a place reserved just for you. And I promise, once you meet Him there, you'll never settle for less than His best again.

-2-

Is Love Supposed to Hurt?

MAYBE YOU'VE BEEN LOOKING for the perfect man but concluded he's a phantom—a fantasy as elusive as a four-leaf clover. Maybe you've given up on love and settled for mediocrity. Or maybe you've been burned or disappointed in previous relationships, but you feel compelled to keep looking. Whatever the state of your romantic situation, if your happiness depends on a relationship or the hope for one, this book holds good news for you.

Before we go any further, I want you to know this book is not just for women who have fallen into sexual sin like I did. Whether it's inside or outside the covenant of marriage, the motive for many women who struggle with sexual sin is not always for physical gratification. For many women, sex is a vain attempt to obtain affection and affirmation. We trade our bodies for love.

Of course, there are many other things we trade for love. Besides the "friends with benefits" barter that so many of us have used to disguise our need for intimacy, we often use other invisible currencies to get what we want out of relationships. We give flattery to receive affirmation. We trade companionship in hopes of gaining confidence. We compromise for acceptance and approval, and we submit to seduction in exchange for security. Unfortunately, the exchange rate is not even. The price we pay for these negotiations leads us into a downward spiral of destruction and disappointment.

Even so, we overextend ourselves. We give too much too fast. Before we know it, we find ourselves emotionally consumed with the identity, approval, and affection our love interest provides.

For Connie, it wasn't until her second marriage ended that she looked at her relationship patterns. "My childhood was full of verbal abuse. I loved my father, but 'Are you stupid?' was a putdown I heard my whole life," she said. "Needless to say, I gravitated toward men who verbally abused me. I found myself searching for their approval to make up for my father's lack of approval, but nothing I did was ever good enough."

I can relate to Connie's situation. My own father put me down, although it was in a more subtle way. Whenever I expressed a dream he felt was out of my reach, he sharply rebuked me. "You can't do that!" he warned. I knew my father was only hoping to spare me unnecessary disappointment, but I believed him. I became a young woman who doubted she could accomplish anything. Consequently, I settled for less than I desired. I believed good things and good relationships were only for others, not me.

WHEN TWO HEARTS COLLIDE

I was in my last semester of graduate school studying for my master's degree in business administration when I met Tom. I was twenty-four and he was twenty-seven. He still lived at home and didn't have a job. His high school diploma was no match for my book-smart brain, but I saw so much potential in him. I was captivated by his charm and the stories he told. Enthralled, I listened to him talk for hours. He had a hard life and struggled with drug addiction for twelve years, but he had been sober for almost three years. Like a rescue worker, I felt compelled to help this injured soul.

"Why don't you take it slow?" my dad cautioned. "What's the rush?"

Instead, wedding plans began.

Full of hope and anticipation, I carried a list of expectations into my marriage longer than a child's Christmas list. When my expectations were unmet, I became angry and bitter. I thought marriage would make me happy. Instead, Tom and I fought constantly. Tom started his career in sales, which came with a few perks that he especially enjoyed—sleeping in and setting his own hours. I expected an eight-to-five lifestyle, so when he woke up late and sauntered off to work late in the afternoon, I found myself about as close to crazy as I've ever been.

> *Like a rescue worker, I felt compelled to help this man's injured soul.*

It didn't take long for the bills to pile up. Two months after the birth of our first child, Brittany, we received an eviction notice. We moved in with Tom's family and fortunately, a few months later, I got a job with the Federal Reserve Bank and we moved to Kansas City. I thought a fresh start would enable me to leave my problems in Oklahoma City, but I was wrong. My emotional baggage made the journey right along with my household goods.

During my employee orientation, I noticed that my benefit package included an employee assistance program, which offered up to four sessions a year with a family therapist. *Finally, someone to fix my husband,* I thought as I scheduled my first appointment. About the only thing I remembered from my mini-rehab was the therapist's theory on problems: "Imagine that your issues are helium balloons," he said. "Just let them go." I clutched my issues tighter. I couldn't fathom how to let go of the strings.

Still desperate for relief, I begged Tom to go to church. As soon as we found a congregation we both agreed to join, I insisted we go to marriage counseling. Pastor Dan agreed to meet with us weekly. *Maybe he can fix Tom,* I hoped.

The problems in our marriage were building up steam, and I was about to bust. I had suspicions Tom was using drugs again, but I was so focused on his issues that I was clueless about my own need for healing. I was a desperate woman looking for a fix. The only problem was that I wasn't a drug user—I used men. For me, the thrill of a new relationship had always been intoxicating.

One Monday in early fall, my work team headed out of town on a bank exam. Sitting in the back seat of the car, I stared out the window. Tiny tornadoes herded crimson and burnt-orange leaves along the fence lines. My heart felt thrashed by the wind as well. Away from familiar surroundings, the enticement to let it all out was more than I could bear. I wasn't the promiscuous type. I didn't set out to have an affair. All I really wanted was to forget my pain and anguish. I thought my fantasies were a harmless way to relieve my anger. But as the day progressed, my "mind affair" escalated.

Situated at the bar after work, stirring my cute little cocktail like I had seen the women on *The Love Boat* do, my inhibitions took a vacation. When Mr. Handsome sat on the barstool next to me, I was vulnerable prey.

The next morning, I stood in front of the mirror and looked at my red eyes. Tilting my head back, I squeezed eye drops into my eyes. *What have I done?* A twinge of guilt accompanied my hangover. But as soon as I shoved it aside, I realized I no longer felt anger. In fact, I could actually smile. In a sick way, the affair was my revenge. My payback. For a while, I felt refreshed and able to deal with issues I couldn't face before.

But like a drug addict, I needed increasing doses to get the same escape from reality. Two more one-night stands followed, and then an ongoing affair with an old college sweetheart. I was not proud of myself. I certainly didn't tell my friends. I especially hid my shame at church. After all, if you've got Jesus, you should have it all together, right?

> *Like a drug addict, I needed increasing doses to get the same escape from reality.*

It was getting harder and harder to keep up the charade. Caught up in the affair with my old boyfriend, something was different this time. The measure of relief I initially found from my escape from reality was not the same measure I felt now. Something had shifted. I felt lured into a trap I couldn't escape. The numbness had worn off and the pain was excruciating.

I knew that the way I was dealing with my anger was just a momentary reprieve, but it was the only relief I could find. I told my pastor about the affairs in a private session. At one point, I told him, "If you can get through to my husband, if only he would change, I can get better."

My pastor understood my frustrations about the marriage, but he wasn't buying my blame.

"Christy," he said, "I realize your husband has issues, but so do you. And the only way you will ever recover is to confess your adultery to your husband. As long as you keep this stronghold cloaked in secrecy, you will never be free. Not that I think spousal confession is always the best route, but I've given this a lot of prayer. And in your case, your husband needs to know. It's the only way to ensure that you break the cycle of addiction."

Stunned, I countered, "Addiction? Are you kidding? My husband is the one with the problem! What are you talking about?"

"Christy, without a full disclosure, you will continue to be defeated in this area. This sin will always be a threat to you unless your confession is complete. Proverbs 28:13 says that 'He who conceals his sins does not prosper, but whoever confesses and renounces them finds mercy.' I've counseled a lot of married couples. I don't always recommend that infidelity is disclosed to the spouse, but I'm afraid in your case, due to the amount of pain involved, you won't be able to fight future temptations and successfully renounce your sin unless you completely burn the bridge by full disclosure. At some point, you will have to tell Tom."

As far as I was concerned, there was no way that was ever going to happen.

By now the shame that could have caused me to repent was buried far beneath my anger. I felt betrayed and trapped. Broken dreams and empty promises strangled me in misery. As the noose of his addiction and deceit tightened, I justified my affairs.

He deserved it.

He should have seen it coming.

What I didn't realize was that I would be blindsided too—by a ricochet of my own issues. Not long after I confessed to Pastor Dan, Tom had an individual session for counseling. Apparently, he was beginning to have suspicions.

When Tom confronted me, I felt cornered with nowhere to hide—nowhere to escape the pain and misery. I had been running on the edge of reality, and like an errant basketball player, I was caught out of bounds.

And now I was benched.

I'd only known pain in love. When the pain of one relationship grew too intense, I ran to another. I was a relationship addict who couldn't break free on her own.

Getting busted was the worst *and* the best thing that ever happened to me. For the first time in my life, I had nowhere to run but straight into the arms of Christ. I wasn't sure I could even breathe without my drug. But once it was confiscated, there was nowhere to go but up. Solitary confinement with no access to my drug was exactly where Jesus wanted me. From there, it wasn't long before I began to learn how women like me got to that point.

WE GRAVITATE TOWARD WHAT IS FAMILIAR

Psychologists tell us that much of our self-image is formed in early childhood through our experiences and our perception of how others judge us. If these experiences and perceptions are negative, we assume the blame. When we don't heal from the shame, we may carry wounds into adulthood that create a self-fulfilling prophecy. In his blog post *Repeating Patterns in Relationships*, Wes Hopper explains that this is why so many of us who grow up with criticism "subconsciously look for someone who's critical so we can be good enough to get their approval."[1]

> **Sometimes we unknowingly commit to misery because it's all we know.**

There are a host of other negative circumstances that shape our identity and cause us to be attracted to unhealthy relationships. Maybe you grew up with abuse, addiction, ridicule, or neglect. If so, you might be subconsciously drawn to relationships with men who are controlling or abusive, have addiction issues, belittle you, or are emotionally distant or physically unavailable. Or maybe your father was absent due to divorce or his job situation. If so, you may be drawn to men who are emotionally unavailable. Sometimes we unknowingly commit to misery because it's all we know.

When we crave approval, attention, affection, or love, it's easy to think that a relationship will satisfy our craving. That's normal because we were created for companionship. The book of Genesis tells us when God created us, He desired to be so close to us that He breathed His very life into us. Genesis 2:7 says, "And the Lord God formed man of the dust of the ground, and breathed into his nostrils the breath of life; and man became a living soul."

When my children were babies, I rocked them to sleep. In their peaceful slumber, I cherished the feeling of their breath against my cheek. I think God longs for that same closeness and intimacy with us. His presence is meant to sustain our very life. In fact, we didn't become a living soul until God breathed His life into us.

He designed a place inside of us, our inner man or spirit, as a place where we can enjoy intimacy and fellowship with Him. This space is like a vacuum that longs to be filled. The problem is that it is so easy to fill this place with inferior substitutes.

Our Creator longs to satisfy our emotions and passions, our desires and appetites, with His life-giving breath, but He wants to be our first love. Dissatisfaction comes when we allow human relationships to invade the place that is intended for divine intimacy.

Until we allow Christ full occupancy, we're naturally drawn to fill our own soul. We'll inhale approval wherever we can find it. When we fill the place meant for His devotion with human intimacy, however, we settle for a counterfeit oneness that prevents our true contentment and joy.

What about you? Does your happiness depend on being in a relationship or marriage? Do you feel stuck? Do you tend to gravitate toward the same type of men—guys who are emotionally unavailable, controlling, abusive, or needy? When you're unhappy, do you find yourself fantasizing about your next relationship? Do you commit too soon because of "chemistry"? Are you afraid of being alone? Have you settled for an unhealthy relationship because it's better than not having one?

If you answered yes to one or more of these questions, you might be addicted to love. You might be a love junkie.

WHAT IS A LOVE JUNKIE?

A love junkie is a woman who is addicted to unhealthy relationships. A love junkie often chooses the same type of man over and over again, all the while knowing these men are wrong for her. Love junkies are not lacking in knowledge about the unhealthy nature of these relationships, yet saying no doesn't seem like an option. Compelled by an invisible magnet back to the same familiar pain, love junkies allow repeat offenders to take advantage of their emotions and bodies. They are easily manipulated due to their generous and often overly responsible natures.

Most love junkies settle for less than they desire. They may allow men to belittle them and emotionally abuse them. Instead of walking away, they justify and minimize their man's behavior in order to excuse and validate chaos. For many, it's like being caught in quicksand—before they realize the danger, they're in too deep.

If you are a love junkie, chances are you trade sex for affection. (Yes, even Christian women.)

You jump through hoops for approval.

You wear yourself thin for affirmation.

Don't get me wrong. Affection, approval, and affirmation are legitimate needs. You deserve to have a healthy relationship or marriage with a man who is healthy enough in his soul to provide these. And if you choose not to be in a romantic relationship, you deserve to be completely content without one. The point is, if you're a love junkie, you're caught in a destructive cycle that has wounded your soul. The good news is whether you are in a romantic relationship or not, you can walk in the freedom of Christ and be whole and complete! Your recovery is up to you.

HOW BADLY DO YOU WANT FREEDOM?

In *Kissed the Girls and Made Them Cry*, author Lisa Bevere writes about a call she received from a mother who was concerned about her daughter's sexual involvement with a dangerous man. The mother had asked Lisa to speak with her daughter. Lisa writes, "I was rather doubtful. I learned long ago when people know right from wrong and still choose wrong, you can talk and pray with them until you are blue in the face but nothing changes until there is a change of heart."[2]

Seeing the problem is only the first step to healing. No matter how badly others want our freedom, we have to want it. We have to desire freedom. We have to saturate ourselves in the promise of freedom and leave our problems behind.

In my own life, I'm sure others saw my problems long before I was aware. I was so focused on my first husband's faults that I was oblivious to my own. I had fallen for the lie that my relationship was the source of my happiness. I was miserable and desperately needed to change, but it wasn't until I was willing to face my issues that recovery was possible.

FINDING FREEDOM

The best way to improve the health of our relationships is to improve our own soul health. As long as our contentment is tied to someone else's behavior, we hand over the reins to our happiness to someone else. The only way to ensure our own peace is to take responsibility for our own well-being and to eliminate toxic behaviors that destroy our joy and threaten our stability. Why is that so important? Because we attract who we are.

> *The best way to improve the health of our relationships is to improve our own soul health.*

Can we change the foundation of our relationships? Can we develop healthy communication and trust? Is it possible to find satisfaction in love? I say yes, and in the chapters ahead, I will show you how.

By applying the steps to breaking the toxic love cycle in this book, you can improve the health of your own soul *and* dramatically improve the health of your relationships as well. Many singles I've worked with have implemented these steps and have dramatically changed the kind of relationship they get in to. Married women I mentor have discovered faulty beliefs and replaced them with solid scriptural truths. As a result, intimacy abounds in their marriages.

The steps and practices are based on simple biblical truths. Yes, I did say simple, but *simple* doesn't always mean *easy*. I'm not going to sugarcoat this. It will take perseverance and determination to repair the damage to your soul. But one step at a time, you can get there. You can learn how to guard your heart and change the behaviors that have caused you to gravitate toward unhealthy relationships.

Love Junkies will unravel some of the biggest lies that keep women bound in unhealthy relationship patterns. But recognizing the problem is only the beginning. Many of us understand why we make certain relationship mistakes, but we lack the wisdom to make necessary changes. In order to eliminate the baggage, we have to replace the lies with a strong foundation based on scriptural principles. I love the promise from Proverbs 2:10: "For wisdom will enter your heart, and knowledge will be pleasant to your soul." When we consistently apply God's wisdom to our own understanding, the greatest opportunity for change can occur.

I also love the promise of Proverbs 3:13: "Blessed is the man who finds wisdom, the man who gains understanding." Other versions say, "Happy is the man who finds wisdom and joyful is the person who finds understanding." Any way you look at this verse, the promise is blessing, happiness, and joy.

Based on the acronym IF-I-PRAY, the seven steps to breaking the toxic love cycle that you'll learn in this book are:

+ **Identity**: the practice of seeking your worth through the reflection of Christ and not the opinions of others.

+ **Forgiveness**: the practice of cleansing your soul of toxic waste by choosing to walk in forgiveness.

+ **Imagination**: the practice of maintaining a healthy thought life so you can follow God's vision for your future.

+ **Prayer**: the practice of conversing with God to seek direction and wisdom.

+ **Resolve**: the practice of adding divine revelation to your human strength.

+ **Accountability**: the practice of protecting your will by surrendering your choices to wise counsel.

+ **Yes**: the practice of surrendering your will and allowing God to lead and guide your life.

Each step will describe the behavior and character traits of someone who excels in its practice. Scriptures will support why each step is biblically relevant. You'll also have access to an online soul assessment—a self-assessment tool to help you evaluate your strengths and weaknesses. It's especially important to identify our areas of weakness so we can put measures in place to protect our vulnerability. After you take the assessment, note the areas you want to improve. To make that achievable as you study each step to breaking the toxic love cycle, you'll find several hands-on ways to apply the principles through strategic exercises or "action points" specifically designed to help you improve your soul-health in that area. You'll discover that as you change your habits, your soul can experience tremendous healing. You'll learn how to ditch the drama that often comes with romantic relationships and find the contentment you've always wanted.

— 3 —

What is Relationship
Addiction?

RELATIONSHIP ADDICTION is an attempt to quench
our hunger for spiritual intimacy with the approval and affection we receive through romantic relationships—either real or
imagined. Relationship addiction does not always entail a sexual
relationship, but an emotional fixation is usually present.

Bill Urell, addiction therapist and author of numerous articles
on recovery, says this: "An addictive relationship is an unhealthy
situation in which you suffer cravings for the attention and presence of another person. It can lead to feelings similar to drug
withdrawal if these needs are not met, including low self-esteem,
helplessness, lack of self-confidence and passive behavior."[3]

In the quest for intimacy, a relationship addict substitutes
the use of romantic relationships to provide a counterfeit comfort and oneness. Trading the affections of men for affirmation
and trying to substitute romance for spiritual intimacy will never
satisfy. It ultimately leads to disappointment because an earthly
relationship can't fulfill a heavenly role. A boyfriend, fiancé, or
spouse will never fulfill the role of Christ in our lives.

Lisa Bevere writes about her college experience before she accepted the love of Christ: "When I walked into my classes or around the campus, I was flirted with, whistled at, or asked out. All the attention made my head spin, because I had known mostly name calling and jeers during the previous four years. I pretended to handle it well, but inside I was shaky and unsure of myself. I began to find strength by drawing male attention, even though at one level it frightened me."[4]

The lack of knowledge about how to develop a healthy relationship coupled with Lisa's strong need for affirmation caused her to embrace the liberal extremes of campus culture. In one semester, Lisa dated more than forty-five guys.

Unfortunately, with the way movies, television shows, and other media have influenced our culture with hyper-sexuality and instant relationships, many women may not understand how destructive it is to go out with so many men. In fact, many young women think that dating a multitude of men is part of the college experience. But when we embrace the standards of our culture, we are headed for disaster. Although the Bible does not specifically address the concept of dating, Proverbs 12:26 tells us that a righteous woman is cautious in friendship. There is no way to be cautious in friendship when you're going out with several men at once or going out with men with whom you are barely acquainted.

BOND OR BONDAGE?

Lauren has always rushed into relationships. When she met Tyler, she ignored his controlling behavior and the way he isolated her from family and friends. Soon, she was trapped in a vicious cycle of manipulation and emotional abuse followed by profuse apologies and showers of affection. In the past three years, Lauren has broken up with Tyler more than five times, but can't seem to stay away. Tyler's charm always convinces her that he has changed.

"Tyler was so attentive in the beginning," she said. "I fell in love almost immediately. By the time I started to notice how controlling he was, it was too late. Besides, I was certain he would change."

I was certain he would change. How many times have you heard that come out of the mouth of one of your girlfriends? Or out of your own mouth? Women are nurturers. We long to help, especially when we think it is within our power to change someone. The power of romance is strong enough to block all reason. Romance trumps reason because it can be deceptive.

> *The power of romance is strong enough to block all reason. Romance trumps reason because it can be deceptive.*

The apostle Paul warns us: "I urge you, brothers, to watch out for those who cause divisions and put obstacles in your way that are contrary to the teaching you have learned. Keep away from them. For such people are not serving our Lord Christ, but their own appetites. By smooth talk and flattery they deceive the minds of naive people" (Romans 16:17).

Lauren was deceived by Tyler's flattery. She recognized that he did things that bothered her, but since she was already emotionally connected, her discernment was compromised and she lacked the resolve to do the right thing—run away.

Lauren made the mistake that a lot of women make—jumping in emotionally way too soon. She was looking for intimacy, but that's not what she got. Her emotions blinded her ability to judge and perceive. As Shannon Ethridge writes, "Be careful not to mistake intensity for intimacy. Intensity fades as the newness wears off, but intimacy continues to blossom the longer you know a person."[5]

Jeremiah 17:9 says, "The heart is deceitful above all things and beyond cure. Who can understand it?" If our heart is beyond cure, how can we succeed in love? If our heart will deceive us, how can we ever make wise choices with romance?

Idealistic wisdom tells us to follow our heart, but is that what Scripture tells us? Does Scripture advocate making decisions about our life with our emotions and passions? Do we make choices concerning our future with our own understanding? If so, why do we need the wisdom contained in the Word of God if we can make intuitive decisions?

Because we can't make wise decisions with our emotions and our own reasoning. Jeremiah 17:7 tells us that "blessed is the man who trusts in the Lord, whose confidence is in him." The more we make decisions based on wisdom instead of our emotions, the more successful our relationships will be. Emotions waiver and change, but the wisdom of God is our anchor.

Aubrey wishes she had used wisdom instead of her own reasoning in her relationship with Darrell. When they first started dating, Aubrey caught Darrell in a few lies.

"He lied about silly things, like when he mailed a package—trivial things that really weren't significant," Aubrey said. "But I chose to ignore it from day one, because he was a Christian, and it looked like he had everything else going for him. I had this tunnel vision of what I wanted in a man and figured no one was going to be perfect."

Aubrey and Darrell spent several months dating and began discussing a possible future together. "As time went on, the lies got bigger," she said. "It got to the point that I couldn't trust him about anything. When I confronted him, he'd twist the issue to make it look like it was my fault and interrogate me about why I didn't trust him. I wish now that I would have listened to my gut in the beginning."

Proverbs 14:15 says, "The gullible believe anything they're told; the prudent sift and weigh every word" (The Message). No wonder we run into so much misery. It's time to stop believing everything men say and pay closer attention to their actions, which are a more reliable measure of integrity and character.

Any man can make verbal claims about his reliability and honor, but words are cheap. Proverbs 26:24 warns us: "A malicious man disguises himself with his lips." So let's make up our mind to wait. Resolve to be patient and not get in a hurry emotionally. In time, a man's actions will either confirm or deny his claims.

In *Finding the Love of Your Life*, Neil Clark Warren says, "Our society—specifically, television and the movie industry—teaches people to rely almost exclusively on their 'natural instincts' when choosing a mate. But romantic feelings, those seemingly trustworthy emotions, offer almost nothing of substance when it comes to making a wise choice about a potential marriage partner. In fact, they frequently get in the way. They literally anesthetize you to the critical factors you desperately need to examine."[6]

In relationships, it's wise to set our emotions aside and focus on facts. Our emotions will trick us into believing that what we are feeling is real. Often, we'll minimize distasteful actions and ignore things that we would otherwise consider unacceptable. Lauren wished she had followed this wisdom.

> **Before you release your heart to love, you need to make sure that the object of your affections is worthy of your trust.**

"I remember the first time Tyler hit me," Lauren continued. "It had never happened before so I didn't see it as a pattern. I broke up with him several times after he got violent, but we always ended up back together. One time we broke up and I moved away. It lasted a couple of months before I couldn't stand it anymore. I packed my things and headed back to Texas—back to the relationship. The night before, I had a dream. He was pulling me close to kiss me. I resisted, but he was stronger. When he kissed me, a vibration like a rattlesnake went all through me, and I felt an evil presence inside of me. I know now that this dream was a warning from God to not go back to him, but I went anyway."

Lauren's story may be more extreme than yours. Not all women who suffer from relationship addiction experience emotional or physical abuse like Lauren, but most will experience a deep dissatisfaction with the relationship. Relationship addiction causes women to notice problems with their partners but feel helpless to change them, so they accept unacceptable behavior. They compromise their values and expectations in a relationship in order to have their emotional needs met. In the process, they fail to see what's wrong with themselves.

"I've had other boyfriends," Lauren told me. "I've also had other problems like alcohol abuse, but I call Tyler my strongest addiction." Lauren had been hooked. She allowed her emotions to dictate her behavior and now that she was irresistibly attracted to Tyler, she was unable to break it off with him. She knew in her heart the right thing to do, but she lacked resolve to act on that wisdom.

Lauren's story is an example of why it is so important to guard our hearts. Shame, inadequacy, and delusions of self-sufficiency prevent us from realizing how vulnerable we are. Our hearts deceive us into believing that we should be strong enough to handle the temptations of romance on our own. Proverbs 22:5 says, "In the paths of the wicked lie thorns and snares, but he who guards his soul stays far from them." Discernment is often ironic: those who need it think they already have it, while those who have it realize they need more.

Your heart is your most valuable asset. Before you release your heart to love, you need to make sure that the object of your affections is worthy of your trust. If you give away your love too freely, it is difficult to walk away, even when you know you should.

Lauren admitted she needed help. "I saw the pattern," she said. "We get back together, we fight, I leave. At first I'm strong, but when the bad memories and pain subside, my strength fades. Three months is about as long as I've made it before getting back on the merry-go-round."

Aubrey ended her relationship with Darrell, but by the time she decided to break it off, the hurt was deep. Lately, Aubrey's been doing some soul searching. "I've been asking God to show me what it is about myself I don't value," she said. "Why do I think I only deserve a mediocre relationship?"

Aubrey is onto something with that question. When we really believe we deserve a godly, romantic relationship with a foundation of trust and respect, it's easier not to compromise. Of course, not all the red flags we notice are deal breakers. Obviously, some are, but red flags are definitely a warning to slow down, set our emotional responses aside, and assess things from a more rational viewpoint.

HOW DID WE GET HERE?

The epidemic of relationship addiction in our culture is obvious. Cultural influences that put emphasis on sex and romance have eroded the moral fabric of our society. Women's magazines contain ads that would have been considered pornographic just two decades ago. Our children are "going out" in grade school, and we think it's cute. Nine-year-old McKenzie complained to her mother, "At my school, if you want to be popular, you have to have a boyfriend *and* kiss him. Plus, you have to cuss. Otherwise, you can't be in 'the club.' My friends talk about boys *all* the time. Why can't we just play?" It's alarming that young girls are exchanging their bodies for attention before they've put away their Barbie dolls.

The requirements for fitting in can be way too much for young girls to handle, and yet, in order to be accepted, many of them "pay their dues." Compromising in grade school paves the way for larger compromises in middle school, high school, and eventually college. Children are having sex at incredibly young ages, and sex before marriage is now considered the norm, even for Christians. Divorce is rampant and relationships are replaced before the judge pounds the divorce gavel.

Sin is progressive and creeps in little by little. Jesus taught this principle in Matthew 26:41: "Watch and pray so that you will not fall into temptation. The spirit is willing, but the body is weak." When we allow sin in moderation, we get familiar with it and eventually become desensitized. Hollywood sells chick-flicks and romance like Reese's sells peanut butter and chocolate. Romance and sex are often thought of as a package deal.

The obsession with romance is a product of our culture, which has changed dramatically over the last century. What was considered normal behavior for women one hundred years ago seems foreign to this generation.

Who is paying the price? We all are. We all carry the burden of a broken generation. Women are suffering from the pain of broken dreams and broken hearts. Children's lives are split between two homes as almost one out of two children are deprived of living with their natural father. Grandparents are raising their grandchildren at a time when they should be enjoying retirement. Unfortunately, sin takes us further than we want to go, keeps us longer than we want to stay, and costs us more than we want to pay.

THE EVOLUTION OF THE LOVE JUNKIE

For many reasons, the need for recovery from relationship addiction has never been greater. Due to the divorce rate, many young girls do not get the love they need from a father figure. Their natural instinct often compels them to replace the lack of fatherly love with a romantic relationship. Furthermore, media obsession with romance promotes the idea that intimacy can be microwaved, portraying an unrealistic picture of how a true relationship develops.

The internet has facilitated rampant growth of relationship addiction. Access to millions of profiles makes finding a relationship as easy as surfing the web. Finally, deterioration in the moral values of our country has made sex before marriage so common that purity is almost a joke. Television and Hollywood have popularized sexuality to the point that girls as young as nine and ten are already dressing seductively.

Why is the issue of relationship addiction so unnoticed? Many reasons. Marriage is the backbone of our society. Relationships are socially expected and socially acceptable, so it's hard to notice when the compulsion is out of control. The hurt lingers. Everyone wants to be loved, and that's a good thing. But when our need for intimacy and approval is not met by God, most of us will find other ways to fulfill our needs. Whether we are married or single, the hunger pangs of approval drive many people into relationship addiction. If we add to social expectations for relationships the standards that the church holds for marriage, the propensity to be in a relationship is even higher. The church has held marriage up so high that many singles feel incomplete and broken when not in a relationship. It's as if the church has made marriage and family an idol.

Our craving for acceptance holds us captive even when the bond is toxic.

The social effect and cultural responses from years of subliminal saturation is that Christians have adapted to the mindset of the world. There has been an evolution. We are supposed to be separate, but we are becoming common descendants with the world. Sadly, divorce statistics for Christians are not lower than those for non-Christians. The sanctity of marriage has been jeopardized, and we are passing the cultural mindset on to our children who are embracing our mistakes as their reality. How can we escape the bondage?

When the pain becomes unmanageable, we need a diagnosis. God can't heal what we won't reveal. Thomas Edison once said, "Restlessness and discontent are the first necessities of progress." Once we pinpoint the issues, there comes a bit of calm. At least we can identify the problem. At least we know what's wrong. Now we can work on finding a solution.

ARE YOU ADDICTED TO RELATIONSHIPS?

Many women run from relationship to relationship. Our craving for acceptance holds us captive even when the bond is toxic because the need for the affirmation a relationship promises can be very powerful. The resulting high is intoxicating and the addiction is real. The following is a list of typical symptoms of relationship addiction. Read through the inventory and identify the symptoms apparent in your behavior:

+ You can't imagine not being in a relationship. If you aren't in one, you are looking for one.

+ You leave one unhealthy relationship only to find yourself drawn back into another one just as toxic.

+ You are easily manipulated. You often fall for what men say and ignore what they do.

- Although you desire a man to be the spiritual leader, you often compromise your faith or settle for men with whom you are not equally yoked (2 Corinthians 6:14).

- You don't see character flaws until you're in too deep.

- You think God is going to use you to change your partner or spouse.

- A false sense of guilt makes you feel overly responsible for others.

- You give in to sexual temptation even when you only want affection.

- Your commitment is more important than your pain.

- You cater to the needs, opinions, and demands of your partner instead of your own.

- You fantasize about how a different relationship would eliminate your current heartache.

- You choose men who don't have the capacity to love or commit.

- You focus on their problems and ignore your own.

- You settle for less than you really want in a relationship.

- You find yourself thinking, *If only he would change, I could be happy.*

How did you do? Go back and look at the behaviors you recognized. While there is no score for this quiz, if the items you pinpointed caused you to realize you have unhealthy behavior in romantic relationships, read on. Remember what I said earlier: The first step to getting soul healthy is to identify our weaknesses.

In the coming chapters, we will learn how our behavior can compromise our spiritual health and jeopardize our relational health. Then we will identify ways we can change our habits so we can enjoy optimal soul health. When our own soul is healthy, a remarkable thing happens to our relationships. If we're single, we gravitate toward healthier relationships, and if we're married, we enjoy a more satisfying marriage with deeper emotional connections.

− 4 −

Emotions Out, Logic In

JOHN D. MOORE, associate professor of health sciences at American Military University and a licensed clinical professional counselor, describes four phases of love addiction in what he titles "The Obsessive Love Wheel."[7] Similar to a merry-go-round, the phases (attraction, anxious, obsessive, and destructive) can repeat cycles over and over again.

Moore describes phase one, the *attraction phase*, as being characterized by an instantaneous and overwhelming attraction to another person, with an immediate urge to rush into a relationship regardless of compatibility.

The strong impulse to move rapidly into a relationship should be a Christian's first clue—a waving red flag—to be extremely cautious. God never rushes us. Satan is the one who wants us to make snap decisions before we have a chance to reconsider. Satan pushes for immediate emotional intimacy, but God intends for relationships to develop gradually. There is a huge difference between lasting love and fleeting emotions. Lasting love takes time and trust to build, but emotions that surface too quickly come in the form of counterfeit intimacy and should be regarded as a false alarm.

In the attraction phase, caution is abandoned, but it's exactly at this point where discretion is most necessary. This is the point where the intoxicating high of romance is the strongest. It's the deceptive hook. We would do well to resist the bait and put our heart on hold. If the relationship is born of God, it will stand the test of time. It's impossible to be certain whether or not the initial chemistry is genuine at the very beginning of a relationship. Only time and the revelation of character will confirm if someone is a safe match. Remember, a wise woman is cautious in friendship, especially romance. As psychologist Neil Clark Warren points out:

> *True compatibility is not based solely on the initial burst of chemistry.*

Some people are addicted to all the excitement that is present in the early phases of the "passion period." Can you imagine any drug-altered state more intense? . . . Like a drug addict constantly in search of his next high, some people simply thrive on supercharged feelings. So they date one person after another, relishing the thrill of soaring emotions—as long as they last. Others go ahead and get married, only to find that the passion abates, sometimes disappearing for long stretches of time. Then they seek the "turn-on" experience in extramarital encounters, pornography, or in some other way. The fact is, these people are addicted to "passion surges," and they need help to get free of their imprisonment.[8]

True compatibility is not based solely on the initial burst of chemistry. In fact, sometimes, there isn't any electricity in the beginning at all. Many couples I've met who build their relationship slowly report that they weren't even attracted to each other in the beginning. Like my friend Monica. "He was okay," she said, describing her boyfriend. When she first met Marcus, he seemed more like a brother than a romantic interest. But the more she got to know him she realized God had brought him into her life for marriage.

"As our relationship grew, so did what I used to call chemistry," Monica added. "And it's never left. I'm more attracted to Marcus now than I ever was to any of the guys that I used to pine for in my single days."

Carol, who has been married to George for over fifty years, describes their relationship in the beginning: "We met in junior high and it was totally platonic. I was at least four inches taller than him through at least the tenth grade. We started out as friends, but by the time his height sprouted, so had our affection for each other."

Chemistry often fades, but a relationship founded on friendship and trust can create a deep emotional bond based on mutual respect that grows stronger as the relationship matures. A bond of trust can last well beyond the initial attraction phase. When God is the foundation of the relationship, the unity between the man and the woman and their Maker creates a three-stranded cord that cannot be broken easily. Ecclesiastes 4:12 explains the concept of a God-ordained relationship: "Though one may be overpowered, two can defend themselves. A cord of three strands is not quickly broken." A spiritual union cements the relationship so that it is more able to withstand adversity, conflict, and age.

Even though arranged marriages are not common in our culture, it's hard to deny their success. The divorce rate in arranged marriages is almost nonexistent. Why is this so? I believe it's because partners in an arranged marriage learn how to grow in love. While the feeling of falling in love diminishes over time, the intimacy created by growing in love increases over time.

Unfortunately, attraction in an unhealthy relationship is short lived. Gary Thomas, author of *Sacred Marriage*, explains, "Infatuation can initially feel like it approaches this God-love, but eventually it fades, disillusionment sets in, and the once 'fabulous' relationship soon becomes an excruciating prison."[9]

If we base our hope for the relationship entirely on the feelings we experienced at the beginning phase, expecting those euphoric emotions to be the foundation of love, we are likely to be sorely disappointed. Satan has counterfeits for everything, especially love. If he can lure us into romance and deceive us into building a relationship on a foundation of infatuation and chemistry, it won't be long before he has us exactly where he wants us—in the middle of chaos. We will have settled for his imitation of intimacy—bondage rather than a bond.

The second phase of the Obsessive Love Wheel is the *anxious phase*. "This relational turning point usually occurs after a commitment, whether real or imagined," Moore writes. "The relationship addict creates the illusion of intimacy, regardless of the other person's true feelings." At this point, negative behaviors of the relationship addict begin to emerge and include some or all of the following: unfounded suspicion of infidelity; fear of abandonment; the need for constant contact (in person or by phone, text, or email); feelings of mistrust, accompanied by depression, resentment, relational tension, and obsessive controlling behaviors.

Phase three in Moore's Obsessive Love Wheel is the *obsessive phase*. This phase is characterized by extreme control tactics with the goal of manipulating a love interest into providing more attention. Finally, phase four is the *destructive phase* in which the relationship issues reach maximum chaos, and the person being controlled typically wants out of the relationship. Often, however, it is at exactly this point that profuse apologies and promises to change are made as the offending partner tries to convince the other to stay.

Once the destructive phase is over, unless the couple breaks up, the cycle begins all over again with the attraction phase. In round two of the attraction phase, profuse apologies rekindle passion, renew attraction, and the chaos is left behind by blind hope. No wonder Lauren felt like she was on a merry-go-round—the cycle revolves on a continuous loop.

Gary Thomas provides insight into the phenomenon of sexual chemistry: "The attraction phase of a relationship only lasts three months." This explains why so many people hop from relationship to relationship. When the initial high wears off, they grow discontent and search for another relationship to bring the passion back, not realizing that infatuation has such a short life expectancy. It also may explain why Lauren kept getting back on the merry-go-round. When the destructive phase was over in her relationship with Tyler, she had a choice to make. She could either exit the confusion or get back on for another ride. She bought another ticket on the Obsessive Love Wheel and it began its second round. When the attraction phase recycled, she thought the honeymoon was back. She forgot the pain. She was deceived into thinking that the passion was permanent.

When the Holy Spirit is not guarding our hearts, we can make some ridiculous choices, especially when it comes to romance. The writer of Proverbs 26 makes an interesting comparison to foolish behavior in verse 11: "As a dog returns to its vomit, so a fool repeats its folly." Fortunately, we can break the cycle.

THE IMPORTANCE OF SOUL-HEALTH

Love junkies often expect their happiness to be tied to a relationship. They may get out of one relationship and vow to wait for God. Without a revelation, however, eventually they jump into the unhealthy cycle of another relationship.

Unless we deal with the root of the issue, the problem grows back like a weed. Growth and healing come when we identify our weaknesses and create a plan of improvement. We've got to quit waiting for our relationships to make us happy. Improving our soul-health will ensure that we stay out of bondage. Unhealthy people attract unhealthy friends and relationships, while healthy people attract healthy friends and mates.

God wants you to prosper in your soul and walk in soul-health. No wonder the word *soul* is used in 432 verses throughout Scripture. Clearly, God is interested in soul-health.

> *When the Holy Spirit is not guarding our hearts, we can make some ridiculous choices, especially when it comes to romance.*

He wants to release you from the captivity of relationship addiction. Are you ready to break your chains of bondage, and put an end to the heartbreaks, disappointment, frustration, and chaos? One of the first steps is clearing clutter from your past.

—5—

Baggage Claim

BUILDING A RELATIONSHIP is a lot like building a house. A strong foundation and sound wiring are essential. Many women have issues with one relationship, and instead of taking the time to build a strong foundation for their soul-health first, they cut corners. Building another relationship seems easier than addressing their own issues. Cutting corners, however, will cause the next relationship to go up in smoke as well. Until you focus on the health of your own soul, you will keep running into problems.

The reason is simple: Baggage attracts baggage.

We all have baggage (memories and emotions from past experiences), but if we don't deal with it, our baggage can keep us in bondage.

Janice's marriage of nineteen years ended when her husband suddenly walked out. Her marriage to Matt had been far from perfect, but Janice thought a loving wife was supposed to be tolerant. That's how her mother had been. When her father was unfaithful, her mother turned a blind eye. His unfaithfulness was easier to ignore than confront. Being tolerant worked for her mom. Her father stayed. Janice assumed that same pattern of "forgiveness" would work for her marriage as well.

"The first time Matt had an affair," Janice recalls, "I couldn't believe it. I thought something was wrong with me. I tried harder to be the woman I thought he wanted me to be—sexier, more attentive. I tended to his every need. I kept the house perfect, made his favorite dinners, and even maintained the yard and the cars so he could relax when he came home from work. I thought if I was perfect he would love me more."

When Matt left, Janice carried the same belief system into her next relationships. Like her marriage, her tolerant behavior only encouraged the men she dated to continue their unacceptable behavior. Dillon was addicted to painkillers. She coddled him more. She thought if she nursed his every need, he would soon want her more than the drugs. Instead, he grew abusive. When they called off their engagement, she entered another relationship within weeks. On the outside, Jack looked like a great catch. His thriving business and exotic vacation "gifts" made him seem like every woman's dream. After two brief months of fantasy, he became extremely controlling. Janice thought submission would make her even more appealing. Instead, his demands grew. "It took the intervention of some very concerned friends to help me break away from Jack," she recalled. "And even though I knew I needed a break from men, I was on Match.com the next week."

A few relationships later, Janice reached her wits end. "I knew something had to change. After my divorce, I'd been through five serious relationships within a year and a half. It was ridiculous. But God used my pain to make it clear to me. The problem wasn't the men I dated—it was me. I had false beliefs that attracted the very type of men I was seeking to avoid. As much as I wanted to deny the truth, I knew that until I chose to work on my own soul-health, I'd never find contentment in a relationship."

It's an age-old pattern. For the Israelites, the journey to the Promised Land took forty years because they couldn't let go of their past. Even though their bondage was cruel and miserable, their murmuring and complaining prevented them from moving into the Promised Land. An eleven-day journey took a lifetime, and everyone who crossed the Red Sea died in the wilderness. They went round and round in the desert and never found their promise.

If you're constantly wishing your boyfriend or husband would change, chances are it's time for you to change. If you wonder why you've struggled with so many relationship issues, it's time to consider that the issues may not be with the men you pick—the problem may be you. Issues are inevitable ... misery is optional.

> *If you're constantly wishing your boyfriend or husband would change, chances are it's time for you to change.*

Like the baggage claim at the airport, unhealthy relationships are like a constant rotation of luggage full of dirty laundry. As soon as one bag goes by, another appears. They may look good on the outside, but inside they're loaded with stinky socks and underwear. Are you tired of hanging out at the baggage claim? It's time to get rid of your baggage and improve your soul-health.

Experts say that most people gravitate toward friends and relationships within a ten-point spread of their IQ. Likewise, in the realm of soul-health, you also attract those with whom you are most emotionally compatible. That can be a good thing or a bad thing—it depends on how much baggage you carry around! Ultimately, we attract who we are, and here's the bottom line: The health of your relationship will rarely exceed the health of the least soul-healthy partner. When you know who you are in Christ, however, you can let go of excess baggage and stop trying to control your relationships.

RELINQUISH CONTROL

"I think I've always had a tendency to try to control circumstances," said Claret. "My mom called me 'the other parent.' When I was growing up, my parents both worked and went to school, so I took care of my younger and older sisters. My parents are still married, but their marriage has never been a good one. My mother is very controlling and my father is distant. More than anything, I wanted to create a different home life as an adult, but somehow I managed to duplicate my childhood home."

> *The only person we can change is ourselves.*

She continued: "My husband and I met at school. Shortly after we were married, I realized he was addicted to pornography and was always on the hunt for something or someone better. As if I wasn't already controlling enough, worrying about what he was hiding from me made me even more neurotic. I read his emails, looked through his receipts, and kept track of his mileage. I was constantly trying to catch him in a lie, afraid that he was doing something behind my back."

After ten years of marriage, Claret and her husband divorced, and she started attending a recovery group at our church. "I'm not minimizing his sin with pornography," she explained, "but I learned not all the problems in our marriage were his fault. Slowly but surely, I began to relinquish control. Now, after a year and a half apart, we have reconciled."

Claret acknowledges that her own growth has been a gradual process. "It still bothers me that he loads the dishwasher wrong," she said, "but I am trying to let go of things like that. I'm trying to remember God is in control and my responsibility is to love God and the people He has put in my life—not run their lives and mine. I'm still not very good at it, but I'm getting better. It's easier when I admit my own imperfections. I spend too much money and eat when I'm not hungry. It's just easier to see his sins than my own. So I am trying to give him the grace that I freely extend myself and that God has lavished on all of us."

Claret learned that even though issues in her marriage were painful and there was obvious sin committed by her husband, she was not without fault. Many of her reactions to circumstances were learned in childhood, and her need to control was rooted in a lack of trust. Ironically, it was through relinquishing control that she found freedom. We can learn a valuable lesson from Claret: The only person we can change is ourselves.

You may be asking how you can change yourself. The first step is to determine exactly where you are and what you need to address.

SOUL ASSESSMENT PROFILE

Have you ever looked in a mirror that magnifies your wrinkles and blemishes fifteen times their normal size? It's not fun to see our imperfections so greatly enlarged, but magnifying them allows us to see clearly so we can fix what needs fixing. It's the same with our issues. They're pretty ugly up close, but it's so much easier to change things when we can see the problem clearly.

So, if you dare, take a deep breath and let's look at our issues up close and personal. We're going to take a hard look at some of the relationship patterns we've developed. To facilitate this, I have created a Soul Assessment Profile, an online tool to help you evaluate your soul-health. The exercise is entirely private and purely for self-reflection. The results will help you identify your strengths and weaknesses in each area of the seven steps to breaking the toxic love cycle: identity, forgiveness, imagination, prayer, resolve, accountability, and yes. Once you target areas of concern, you can set goals for improvement and be well on your way to becoming a soul-healthy woman.

To take the assessment, log on to www.christyjohnson.org and click on the Soul Assessment Profile link. Find a time when you will not be distracted for thirty to forty-five minutes, and answer the questions as honestly as you can. Each question lists typical ways women react to a variety of circumstances. Evaluate each statement and select the response that indicates how you believe you respond. We do heart checks to evaluate the health of our heart. We conduct credit checks to see how we can improve our credit score. Employers complete background investigations to assess our character. This assessment is a way to evaluate the condition of your soul.

I encourage you to take the assessment before you dive into the next chapter. Once you're finished, look over your answers and note the areas you want to improve. If you tend to be overly critical of yourself, don't go overboard and make unrealistic goals to change everything all at once. As the saying goes, the way to eat an elephant is one bite at a time. Improving your soul-health is not about perfection, it's about progress.

You won't receive a score on the Soul Assessment Profile, although you will be able to judge whether your behavior is typically low risk, moderate risk, or high risk. Ultimately, it's up to you to decide which areas of your soul-health are acceptable and which areas need improvement. Taking the assessment now will help you get a "before" snapshot of where you are at this moment. Then later, when you've finished reading the book and have had a chance to apply the fundamentals in each profile chapter, you can retake the assessment to see how your answers differ. I'm praying your "after" snapshot will reflect improvement based on new revelations.

> *The traits of soul-healthy women are not always learned naturally— they are habits we choose to learn.*

In conjunction with the Soul Assessment Profile, the discussion of each step to breaking the toxic love cycle will end with several relevant Scriptures and action points you can exercise to strengthen your soul in that area. The action points are intentional activities you can do to overcome the areas of weakness you have targeted. In regard to your weaknesses, you will have to retrain your soul. That's because the traits of soul-healthy women are not always learned naturally. Soul-healthy habits are something we choose to learn. Throughout the rest of this book, you'll train your soul in these habits so that you can enjoy optimal soul-health and consequently, healthy relationships.

Finally, each profile chapter will end with some questions to ponder. You can use these questions for your own reflection, or if you are reading this book with a friend or a group, these questions will be particularly helpful for shared discussion.

GETTING SOUL-HEALTHY

I'll assume that you went on ChristyJohnson.org to take the Soul Assessment Profile. So now that you have a better idea of the strengths and weaknesses in regard to your soul-health, you are ready to move forward. As you endeavor to renew your mind, you'll naturally begin to take action consistent with your new way of thinking. You'll become a different person in relationships, and consequently, your relationships will be healthier and more fulfilling.

> **Breaking the toxic love cycle is based on your choice to transform your thinking.**

First, you must understand that *you* are responsible for your own happiness and fulfillment in any relationship. You are the only one who can make the choice to do things differently. And by now you should be seeing that the only person you can change is yourself. You can't change your partner.

The good news is that breaking the toxic love cycle is based on your choice to transform your thinking (see Romans 12:2). The health of your soul does not depend on your partner. Each of the love junkie traits we discussed earlier is based on lies and false beliefs, but when you anchor your thoughts on the Word of God, your mind begins a transformation process. The apostle Paul put it this way: "We demolish arguments and every pretension [false belief] that sets itself up against the knowledge of God, and we take captive every thought to make it obedient to Christ" (2 Corinthians 10:5).

This does not mean that you have to accept an unacceptable situation. But *you* can be transformed, and as you are, your transformation *will* evoke changes in your relationship. Sometimes changes occur quickly. Other times, change is more gradual. But don't give up. There is a new day coming. If you are in a relationship and it grows as a result of changes you make in yourself, you can give glory to God for it. And if your relationship dissolves as a result of changes you make in yourself, you are one step closer to being free from the bitterness that has held you captive. Once your eyes are wide open and you take responsibility for making those changes, you will be less and less drawn to the types of relationships that leave you feeling empty and unsatisfied. You will be in the process of transformation.

Beth, a children's pastor and mother of three, shared her struggle with loneliness after her divorce: "I couldn't believe I was single again after twenty-three years of marriage. In my eagerness to be in a relationship, I made many mistakes. For several years, God kept telling me to be patient, to wait on Him and to trust Him. That was hard. I hated being alone, but after several weeks of going to bed at 9:30 and crying myself to sleep, I finally gave up. I said, 'God, searching for my mate is your job. You know my heart.' Within a month, some friends introduced me to Jonathan and two years later, we are happily married. It wasn't until I finally surrendered and realized that a man wasn't my source of happiness that God was able to bring my husband to me."

Before I found my freedom in Christ, I was overly concerned about what others thought about me. I lacked self-confidence and wouldn't express my opinion until I knew what others thought. I couldn't stand the rejection that might come if they had a different outlook than I did. To others, I'm sure I came across as pleasantly compliant, but on the inside, fear and insecurity loomed. Like a chameleon, I blended in to match my environment. Insecure, resentful, and often blindsided, I repeated toxic love patterns, even though I should have known better. I desired to bond with a mate. Instead I was deceived into bondage.

When bondage ties you in knots and twists you in chains, there is a way to break free. Be aware, however, that your recovery will take time and perseverance. You didn't get where you are overnight, but one step at a time you can begin to prosper in your soul. Are you ready to break away from the insecurities and bondage of relationship addiction? If so, it's time to learn the first step to breaking the toxic love cycle—embracing the habit of identity.

– 6 –

STEP NUMBER 1:
Identity

IDENTITY: THE PRACTICE OF SEEKING MY
WORTH THROUGH THE REFLECTION OF CHRIST AND NOT
THE OPINIONS OF OTHERS.

MANY OF US LIVE to please others. We spend a lifetime calculating our own worth through the perceptions of those around us. If we think people have a low opinion of us, we may struggle with low self-esteem. It's also possible to have a faulty, inflated opinion of ourselves. For example, if your self-image is based on your achievements or on others' high opinion of you—not on what God thinks of you—you're tottering on an unstable platform of worth.

Whenever our identity is centered on anything but Christ, we risk identity theft. Lori's story is a good example of this. Married for twenty years, her life looked picture perfect.

"I had it all," said Lori. "I enjoyed a wonderful life with a sprawling house in an affluent neighborhood, luxury vehicles, and a fabulous shopping budget. My children went to an exclusive private school. My husband's career was doing very well when all of a sudden he announced, 'I want a divorce.'"

Lori's reaction? "Those words electrocuted my soul," she recalled. "It would have been easier to survive a 1000-watt shock. My world was stripped out from under me. Within a matter of months, I lost not only my marriage, but my home, my cars, and my income. My lifestyle plunged from extravagant to extra vacant.

"To keep my sanity," she continued, "I taught myself to knit. I had never knitted before, but it was the only thing that kept my mind off the despair. I knitted blankets, scarves, and even washcloths. Little by little, God began knitting the wounds of my heart back together."

> **Whenever our identity is centered on anything but Christ, we risk identity theft.**

Lori recognizes now how God changed her through the crisis: "Looking back, I can see that I was a snob living the extravagant lifestyle. When my world—and fancy lifestyle—got turned upside-down, God stripped me of arrogance and false pride. It took a removal of the exterior in order for God to begin interior reconstruction, but I like who I am now."

Lori's identity had been based on her circumstances and her lifestyle. Unfortunately, without a revelation, many women never understand how faulty their identity is. Other women who are performance driven have similar identity issues.

Rachel, a twenty-five-year-old college student studying accounting at the University of Oklahoma, shares these thoughts: "I have always hated the word *average*. My life has been spent pursuing excellence. If I could only be second best at something, I wanted nothing to do with it. In school, I had the best grades; in my first job, I had the highest sales. My motto: never give the boss a reason to complain. Point me toward the top and watch me go over. The surest way (and almost the only way) to make me dislike you was to come between me and what I intended to achieve. I would succeed, come hell or high water."

She concluded: "Nothing wrong with ambition, but since I wasn't anal about things like sports or games, my hang-up was seen as a virtue. But I wasn't just ambitious, I *had* to succeed. My whole estimation of my worth came from my achievement."[10]

Lori and Rachel's stories are common. Our society places great emphasis on acquisition and achievement. Other women put confidence in their acquaintances and appearance. It's so easy to put our confidence in places other than Christ, but it's not secure. A man-made image can come crumbling down at any point. On the other hand, a Christ-centered identity is shatter-proof. Psalm 118:8 says, "It is better to trust in the Lord, than to put confidence in man."

The Bible doesn't use the words *self-esteem* or *self-image* or *self-confidence*. These are modern-day terms to describe what the Bible refers to as trust, hope, or confidence. While self-esteem, self-image, and self-confidence come from *self*, our true identity, hope, and confidence can only come from God.

IS YOUR IDENTITY COMPROMISED?

Look over the following questions and answer as honestly as you can . . .

+ Do you worry about what others think of you?

+ Do you try to blend in so you don't risk criticism?

+ Do you often deny your feelings when you're hurting?

+ Are you defensive when confronted about sensitive issues?

+ Do you look for ways to give compliments in hopes of pulling praise out of other people?

+ Do you compare yourself to other women and feel insignificant in comparison?

+ Do thoughts about change instill fear?

+ Do you fear rejection, even from those whose opinions don't really matter to you?

+ Are you overly concerned about your appearance, never leaving the house without makeup or wardrobe perfection?

+ Do you minimize problems when they exist, pretending everything is okay even when it's not?

+ Do you avoid certain people socially or at church or work because of what others may think?

Christian women with low self-esteem tend to masquerade in a costume, pretending everything is okay. We have to, or so we think, because we have an identity to protect. What we need to understand is this: When we derive our identity from others we will constantly be looking for a fix—something to give us worth. But just like a drug addict, we often spend more than we can afford to maintain our pseudo-sanity. We struggle to find a guarantee of confidence. We can be shaken at any time.

When your identity comes from God, however, your foundation is secure because His love never changes. Then, when disapproval, rumors, or accusations come, you are not shaken. Your confidence is fixed on Christ. If your children rebel, your opinion of yourself does not change. If your boyfriend or ex-husband or parents reject you, your identity is secure. If you're overlooked for a promotion, your faith does not waiver.

The bottom line is this: If God is for you, no one can be against you (Romans 8:31). When you fully realize this, your personal value will no longer be connected to others. Your self-esteem will no longer be derived from the opinions of others.

How can you grasp this truth? With so many worldly influences trying to capture your attention, what can you do to maintain your confidence in Christ? You start with the truth.

THE POWER OF HEARING, SEEING, AND DOING

Meditating on truth is one of the most powerful resources we have to help us improve our soul-health. The psalmist writes in Psalm 1:2, "[Blessed are those] whose delight is in the law of the Lord, and who meditate on his law day and night." The word *meditate* used in this verse comes from the Hebrew word *hagah*. It's interesting to note that *hagah* doesn't mean just *to think*. Hagah means to mutter, moan, growl, speak, and utter.

The Hebrews were more engaged in the practice of meditation than our culture is today. Before I discovered the true meaning of *meditate*, I thought it meant to sit on the floor yoga-style and hum. I've never been one to sit still for long, so I typically found myself nodding off or falling asleep when I sat down to "meditate" like that. Then I'd have to repent for not being able to focus on Scripture. But when I learned that meditating is so much more than just thinking about Scripture, I began to declare the truths in the Scripture out loud. And my faith exploded. The amount of truth my soul retained was life changing. There's power in the spoken truth, because the Word declared out loud creates life!

Even psychological studies prove this point. A study done at the University of Texas found that people remember:

+ 10 percent of what they read

+ 20 percent of what they hear

+ 30 percent of what they see

+ 50 percent of what they see and hear

+ 70 percent of what they say

+ 90 percent of what they do and say.[11]

According to these statistics, if you simply read this book, you are likely to retain only 10 percent of this material. But if you also declare the truth out loud, you will remember 70 percent. Furthermore, if you put your faith into action and apply the truth to your life, you will remember 90 percent. Benjamin Franklin said, "Tell me and I forget. Teach me and I remember. Involve me and I learn."

Are you ready to move forward even more? In the next chapter we'll see how a woman acts when she knows that her identity is found in Jesus Christ, the lover of her soul and the only one who will never reject her.

-7-

Wella's Story

JESUS ANSWERED, "EVERYONE WHO DRINKS
THIS WATER WILL BE THIRSTY AGAIN, BUT WHOEVER
DRINKS THE WATER I GIVE HIM WILL NEVER THIRST."
(JOHN 4:13)

THE FOURTH CHAPTER OF JOHN gives the account of the woman at the well. The Bible doesn't give her name, but let's call her Wella for short. Wella was a woman desperate for love. So desperate that she was willing to risk her life. She engaged in adultery during a time in which women were stoned for promiscuity. That's some serious hopelessness. But when she met Jesus at the well, she accepted the gift of living water that He offered.

Some women need a whole lot of convincing before they will take a gift, as if refusal of a gift is somehow considered good manners. Not Wella. She didn't say, "That's okay. I can manage." The truth was that she couldn't manage. Her life was a disaster. She needed the living water; her own jar was heavy and cracked. It didn't hold enough water to sustain her for long, so she had to fill it again every day. But when Jesus came along, she threw away the broken vessel. She ditched her water jar for the fountain of life.

Wella didn't just hear the truth—she embraced the truth. Then she took actions that established trust in line with her belief. She left her water jar—the very thing she needed for quenching her thirst—with Jesus. Suddenly, it was no longer essential.

Is your water jar cracked? Do you fill it every day only to find out that everything you filled it with has somehow leaked out? It's time to leave your water jar with Jesus. It's time to accept His gift of living water.

THE DAILY GRIND

Wella acknowledged that Jesus was a prophet (John 4:19), so it was apparent that she knew *about* God. She also believed *in* God, but worship was merely a cultural tradition to her. "I know that Messiah (called Christ) is coming. When He comes, He will explain everything to us." Like so many women, Wella believed that knowing Christ was a future event, something that would happen eventually, but not something that could help her today. Her religion wasn't relevant. It was merely a dead set of rules and a ritual. She believed *in* God, but she didn't yet *believe* Him.

Until Christ revealed Himself to her.

If this scene was in a movie, Christ's response to her would be my favorite line. I get chills every time I read the passage. Imagine the shock she must have felt when Christ spoke the next words.

"I who speak to you am He."

Take a moment and let that sink in. *I who speak to you am He.* Has Christ ever revealed Himself to you like He did to Wella? If so, He did it on purpose. He wants you to *believe* Him, not just believe *in* Him. A relationship with your creator is a prerequisite for life. We need the empowerment He provides. There are problems, issues, and burdens that we are not equipped to carry alone.

Christ reveals Himself to us for a reason. God encounters bring new perspective. Revelation comes for the purpose of transformation. What if you were the woman at the well, seeing Christ for the first time? How would you react?

> *God encounters bring new perspective. Revelation comes for the purpose of transformation.*

Wella was so excited about her conversation with Jesus that she left her water jar and ran back to town. She wasn't afraid to face the people who once shunned her. Her shame evaporated because she found the answer. Wella knew she was different now. She knew Jesus had changed her life, and obviously she was convincing. Many Samaritans believed in Jesus because of her testimony. They believed based on her word alone, and as a result, her credibility was redeemed.

Wella's testimony wasn't an eloquent dissertation. It was uncomplicated and straightforward. "He told me everything I ever did." Transparent simplicity is enough. Pure truth is powerful. After her encounter with Christ, Wella was able to hold her head up and walk away from her past. How? By ditching the shame. Once she received His gift of living water, her identity was redeemed, and her shame disappeared. Shame cannot exist in recovery. I'm praying you also have an encounter with Christ. Once you receive His gift of living water, your shame will evaporate as well. Then it's replaced by a brand new identity, followed by a new future.

THE FACE OF A NEW FUTURE

Wella's eyes were opened that day. She heard *and* believed. She no longer saw herself as a dishonorable reject. She saw herself through the eyes of Jesus. Her one-on-one encounter with the man at the well changed her life.

There are just as many women looking for love in the church as there are outside of the church. And just because you attend church and have received salvation doesn't mean you are delivered. Salvation is instant, but deliverance is a process. We have to have an encounter with Christ because that's what enables us to walk out our deliverance. It's not enough to just know *about* God. It's not enough to believe *in* God. In order to overcome the cravings of a love junkie, we have to *believe* Him.

The woman at the well was a relationship addict. Her addiction progressed to the point of adultery, but instead of pointing out the external sin, Jesus could see straight into her heart. Instead of telling her that she was guilty of adultery, he addressed her situation, as I envision it, like this ...

"Ever since you were young, you craved the affection of your father. In desperation for the hunger you felt, you satisfied it with any relationship you could find. They weren't suitable relationships, but you were desperate to feel loved."

Or maybe He started off by telling her that even though her first relationship was abusive, she didn't have to gravitate to abusive relationships any longer. Maybe Jesus saw that the reason for her illicit relationships was her fear of commitment. Maybe she was abandoned as a child and grew up with an unhealthy view of relationships. In response, she vowed never to give her heart to a man. Or maybe Jesus knew that she had believed some lies about love, and those lies kept her from being fulfilled in relationships. Whatever his approach, she listened. He had her attention and she wanted the promise He made.

He promised her water—living water. If she would accept His gift, she would never thirst for inappropriate relationships again. Jesus would quench her thirst. Her desire for approval, affirmation, and acceptance would be met through a relationship with Him.

I believe when she ran back to town, her shame fell with each stride of her sandals slapping against the dusty ground. Exhilarated and excited, she wanted everyone to see a man who told her everything she had ever done. Actually, everything she had ever done was no secret. The entire town knew about her man-habit. She had several live-in lovers. And there was no telling how many men she slept with before she agreed to share their tent.

But it was the way that Jesus pointed out her sin. He didn't condemn her. He promised her a way out of sin by giving her hope, proclaiming liberty from her pain and showing her the remedy. No one had ever done that. No one had ever believed in her before.

But He did.

There was something about the way He spoke to her. He saw through her, and for the first time in her life, she felt affirmation from her heavenly Father. She felt His presence, and even in her shame, He still embraced her. He didn't run away. He saw her flaws but He accepted her anyway. This was a man who loved her uncondi-tionally. He didn't expect her to be perfect before He offered relationship to her. He even looked past cultural differences. He didn't care what anyone else thought.

> **Ditch your shame and stare into the face of your future.**

When Wella left her water jar at the well, she left her past with it. She no longer needed the faulty sustenance that she once relied on. She had found life. With her mistakes behind her, she felt free to embrace her future. Ditch your shame and stare into the face of your future. His grace freed Wella, and He can liberate you as well.

ELIMINATING COUNTERFEIT INTIMACY

Despite the fact that sexually explicit images are commonplace in our culture, the subject of sex is still taboo in many churches. After all, there are more spiritual things to study and discuss. As a result, a woman struggling with sexual issues may be ashamed to get the help she needs. She may try to deal with her secret in se-clusion. Obviously, the rules in church are different than the rules in the world, but where are the tools to help her overcome? Rules without tools are as futile as a scolding finger. She may know better but not know how to implement the rules. She may feel like a spiritual baby in an adult body facing raging temptations.

How can she get the encouragement and advice to overcome her struggles with sexual temptation?

It's easy to ask for prayer for our health, issues with our children, or problems with finances, but prayer for sexual infidelity? Hardly. It is more acceptable in many church circles to get a divorce than to admit marital infidelity.

"I saw the way my church friends shunned Angela after her divorce," explained Dominique. "Angela had been having an affair, and even though she asked for forgiveness, her friends evaporated after Tony filed for divorce. They talked about her behind her back, and Angela became the church reject. I wasn't about to let that happen to me."

Dominique continued: "After Art and I split up, friends saw me crying and surrounded me with consolations. I didn't tell anyone about my affair. I'm sure things would have been much different if they knew why Art left me."

There are certain prayer requests that women deem too confidential, and when problems are isolated, sin abounds and restoration is not possible.

Where does a Christian woman caught up in adultery turn? While she is struggling with her sin, many times she is not embraced within. Friends and church members urge her to stop, but she doesn't know how. They quit calling. Her shame builds. Broken and rejected, she runs to a well on the outskirts of town. She'll find another place of fellowship. It may be the gym, the mall, or a bar, but she feels compelled to find acceptance somewhere.

To clarify, the need for approval and acceptance is not a sexual addiction. However, a woman trapped in relationship addiction may use sex as a bartering exchange. It may be a trade out, a way to swap physical intimacy for emotional intimacy. A relationship addict will do whatever it takes to get her needs met, even if it means compromising her integrity and moral values.

Our society today promotes sex, but the rules were different in Wella's day. Faced with deadly consequences for adultery, most women probably never dared to break the rules. But this woman did. She was desperate—so desperate that she risked her life for love.

How can we get rid of our unhealthy longing for approval and maintain our sexual integrity? The key to eliminating counterfeit intimacy is to find the approval of the Father. As soon as the woman at the well had the approval of the Father, her shame was erased and she was awakened. She saw her destiny and beauty for the first time in her life. She was even a convincing witness to the people in town, but the disciples didn't get it. And sometimes that's how it is when we have an encounter with the Man at the well. It may not be evident to everyone at first. Jesus' disciples, His ministry partners, were surprised to find Him talking to a woman, but they didn't say anything about it. Instead they encouraged Him to eat. When Jesus said that He had food to eat that they knew nothing about, they just scratched their heads in wonder.

"Did someone bring Him a casserole while we were gone?"

Don't be discouraged if others don't recognize the changes God has made in you right away. Likewise, don't be hard on yourself if your identity change is not instant. Sometimes our deliverance from counterfeit sexual intimacy is a gradual awareness. Transformation is often a process, not a lightning bolt experience. Who knows how long it took the woman caught in the act of adultery to "leave her life of sin"? Was she instantly delivered from her shame or was her recovery gradual? Although we aren't told, one thing is clear—an encounter with Christ can change our life forever. It's not always easy to walk away from habits that have established our life. But God isn't asking you to change your past. He's inviting you to change your future.

Kristen once considered herself a modern-day woman at the well. "It's not that I had that many relationships," said Kristen. "It's just that for the most part, I was immediately sexually intimate in every one of them. Christ became real to me after I had my son. Realizing how much I loved him just for who he is helped me understand how much Christ loves me just for who I am. I never understood that until I

> *Transformation is often a process, not a lightning bolt experience.*

had Brice. Now I understand that I don't have to perform to gain love and affection from a man. My son does absolutely nothing to gain my affection and approval, and yet, I love him completely with the most intense love I've ever felt in my life. I don't want to settle for less than that in a romantic relationship. I've realized I don't have to compromise my sexual integrity to have the comfort of a close relationship."

Many of us are modern-day women at the well. When we are drawn to unhealthy relationships, we often compromise our sexual integrity. Then, ironically, our shame keeps us isolated. Please understand there's no shame in being a woman at the well. The well is where thirsty people go. The well is where the water of life is, where Jesus is, where healing and recovery is. The well is where we find the living water to strengthen our identity. Shall we go there now?

— 8 —

Strengthening Your Identity

"AHA" MOMENTS COME AT VARIOUS points in our lives. Sometimes they are divinely orchestrated by God, and sometimes the light of God's truth finally illuminates a dark corner of our mind and we "get it." It's true that we are more apt to have an awakening when we hit bottom, but we can purposely position ourselves where we can understand God's love for us and gain new perspective on our identity in Christ.

How? Read and meditate on the identity Scriptures below. They will help you as you seek to find your worth through the reflection of Christ and not the opinions of others. Pray and ask the Lord for these truths to sink deep into your soul. In that sense, you'll be diving right into the well of living water.

Then look over the list of "action points" or exercises at the end of this chapter. Choose the action points you think would be helpful to fortify you. Implementing these action points will help you position yourself in such a way that the seed of God's truth can blossom in your soul. Each time you meditate on Scripture, you are watering the truth in your spirit. Each time you exercise one of the action points, you are positioning yourself in such a way that the light of God's Word can promote growth. Through the power of the Holy Spirit, Christ can transform your soul and change your identity.

IDENTITY SCRIPTURE TRUTHS

✦ "My people are ruined because they don't know what's right or true" (Hosea 4:6 The Message).

✦ "So God created man in his own image, in the image of God he created him; male and female he created them" (Genesis 1:27 NKJV).

✦ "Beloved, I pray that you may prosper in all things and be in health, just as your soul prospers" (3 John 1:2 NKJV).

✦ "But blessed is the man who trusts in the LORD, whose confidence is in him" (Jeremiah 17:7). "Blessed [is] the man that trusteth in the LORD, and whose hope the LORD is" (Jeremiah 17:7 KJV). Notice that the King James Version of this verse uses the word *hope* instead of *confidence*. Hope comes from the Hebrew word *mibtach* [miv·täkh'], which means trust, confidence, refuge, an act of confiding, and a state of confidence and security.

✦ "The gullible believe anything they're told; the prudent sift and weigh every word" (Proverbs 14:15 The Message).

+ "With persuasive words she led him astray [stole his confidence so she could control him], she seduced him with her smooth talk" Proverbs 7:21).

+ "Above all else, guard your heart, for it is the wellspring of life" (Proverbs 4:23).

+ "In the paths of the wicked lie thorns and snares, but he who guards his soul stays far from them" (Proverbs 22:5).

+ "My son, do not forget my teaching, but keep my commands in your heart, for they will prolong your life many years and bring you peace and prosperity. Let love and faithfulness never leave you; bind them around your neck, write them on the tablet of your heart. Then you will win favor and a good name in the sight of God and man" (Proverbs 3:1-4).

+ "For it is we who are the circumcision, we who worship by the Spirit of God, who glory in Christ Jesus, and who put no confidence in the flesh" (Philippians 3:3).

IDENTITY ACTION POINTS

Remember, identity is the practice of seeking your worth through the reflection of Christ rather than the opinions of others. If you struggle with identity, try these action points:

Speak the Word

Use the suggested Scriptures above or find your own power verses that minister to you. Declare them out loud by filling your name in the blank. For example, take 2 Corinthians 5:17 and insert your name by saying, "Therefore, if _____ is in Christ, she is a new creation; the old has gone, the new has come!" Changes happen when we declare truth with our lips. Our faith is increased when we speak the truth out loud because the Bible says our faith comes through hearing (Romans 10:17). The more we hear, the more we believe. This exercise may feel awkward, but most change feels funny at first. We have to grow into it. Once your circumstances begin to change by the power of the spoken word, you probably won't notice any more awkwardness.

Declare Positive Affirmations

Make a list of positive affirmations about yourself and declare them out loud. When I first had the revelation about speaking truth over myself, I knew I needed to convince my soul that my opinion mattered. It was extremely awkward at first, but I started saying out loud, "I am worthy." Those words almost made me cringe at first because I felt as if I was lying. To me, someone with a worthy opinion already possessed confidence and influence and I wasn't there—yet. I still lacked confidence, but I couldn't deny that God had convicted me of my need to love myself so I could love others as well. Plus, I recognized that if I didn't believe in myself, no one else would either.

The more I spoke the truth about how God values me and my thoughts and opinions, the more my soul believed it. The more my soul believed the truth, the more my confidence increased. Today, it's no longer awkward to say, "I am worthy." If you feel awkward about declaring truth over yourself, do it anyway. Do it until you believe it. It's worth it!

Exercise Your Faith

Pray and ask God how you can exercise your faith and take action on it. Ask God for specific ways to do this and then exercise and practice what He tells you to do. Even when it feels awkward, do it anyway. Don't despise small beginnings. You'll never lift a fifteen-pound weight if you can't lift a five-pound dumbbell, but the more you exercise the stronger you'll get.

For example, I used to fear rejection. I lacked the self-confidence to even initiate a smile to someone I didn't know because I worried they might not smile back. Consequently, I never looked people in the eye unless they spoke to me first. The exercise the Lord had me do was to take a walk in my neighborhood and practice smiling at people. This was huge for me, but the more I did it, the more my confidence increased. That was over twenty years ago, but now whenever I speak at conferences, I can smile at a thousand people at a time.

Evaluate Your Thoughts

Find a quiet spot and ask the Lord to help you eliminate any negative or toxic thoughts you have about yourself. Take a notebook with you and write down the destructive thoughts. You might also try saying your thoughts out loud. If what you say about yourself is not kind and encouraging, and you wouldn't say it about someone else, don't say it about yourself. Our words create life and have the power to produce death, so it is vital that we retrain our brain with healthy thoughts. Ask the Lord to help you write some positive, life-giving thoughts. Practice saying them out loud and declaring these truths over your life. The more you say them and meditate on them, the more you will come to believe them. Plus, it will become easier for you to spot and replace negative and critical thoughts about yourself.

If you have trouble saying nice things about yourself (we all tend to be self-critical), you might begin by imagining that you are saying something nice about someone else. Sometimes it's easier to see the good in others than it is to acknowledge good things in ourselves. Then write those thoughts down and begin saying those truths about yourself.

Give Yourself a Break

Whenever you goof up, give yourself some grace. You give it to others, so why not acknowledge the fact that you are imperfect and believe you'll do better next time? Tell yourself the same thing you'd say to someone else who goofs up. "It's okay. I know you didn't mean to do that. You'll do better next time." Ask God to forgive you, forgive yourself, and let it go.

Evaluate Friends and Places

Is there an ungodly influence in your life? Do others have bad habits you don't wish to learn? If so, it would be wise to change your friends. Protect your soul by discontinuing friendships with people who are not a good influence. Proverbs 13:20 tells us that the companion of fools suffers harm.

Years ago, in the wake of a broken relationship, I was reading Proverbs 4 when verses 14-15 leapt out at me: "Do not set foot on the path of the wicked or walk in the way of evildoers. Avoid it, do not travel on it; turn from it and go on your way."

That's when the Lord told me not to even drive down 10th Street because it housed one of our favorite hangouts. Why would

God tell me that? Because He knew that every time I went down that street, it made me remember the times my former partner and I spent together. He knew I needed a season of time to let my memories heal. He knew that if I starved my mind from entertaining memories of our romance, eventually my mind would heal and my soul would be healthy again.

What we feed grows and what we starve dies.

God was challenging me to discipline myself so that my temptations were minimized, even if they were mere memories. He was showing me how to detox my mind. Dr. Caroline Leaf, author and brain scientist, says, "Detoxifying your thoughts can be like selecting a book from the shelf in your library of memories, rewriting a page in that book, then placing it back on the shelf, free of toxic thoughts and emotions."[12]

It takes effort at first to form new habits, but we should be diligent to replace anything that reminds us of our past sin. When songs on the radio remind us of our old drinking days, turn the channel. When places remind us of painful relationships, go somewhere else. Memories can trigger destructive thoughts that are not only dangerous, but addictive.

Our brain has ruts like a worn path in a grassy lot. Repetitive thoughts like to travel on familiar paths, but we have to break those patterns to get free because thoughts lead to actions. Quit playing the old tapes that recycle in your head. According to Philippians 4:8, we should think about things that are true, noble, right, pure, lovely and admirable. Put your thoughts to the test. If they don't stand up to Philippians 4:8, train your brain to reject and replace them.

Today I can drive down 10ᵗʰ Street because the wounds of my past have healed, but when they were fresh, memories rehearsed too soon would have caused my wounds to fester. If you struggle in this area, protect your heart. Ask the Lord what He wants you to do to put a guard around your heart. He knows you intimately and wants you to completely heal. He knows the wisdom and strategy that will completely restore your soul.

Avoid Negative People or Environments

Begin to pay attention to your surroundings. Take notice when you are in a negative environment. If others are trying to get you agitated, refuse to argue. Say as little as possible and remove yourself from the place if possible. Proverbs 22:24 says, "Do not make friends with a hot-tempered person, do not associate with one easily angered, or you may learn their ways and get yourself ensnared." Negativity is contagious.

Sometimes we don't notice when we are in a negative environment because it's so familiar to us. We get desensitized by the repetition of arguing and chaos. I once had a family member who wasn't happy unless there was a crisis going on. She was always complaining about this or that. All she needed was an audience—me. Politely, I would nod and offer an "um-hum" or "I know" every once in a while to acknowledge that I was listening. That only encouraged her to continue the drama.

I hated getting cornered by her. At times I tried to offer solutions to her problems, but she'd just talk over me. She didn't want any advice. She wanted to be negative.

One day I decided that no matter how awkward it felt, whenever she started complaining, I wasn't going to say a word. It was probably one of the hardest things I ever did. It went against everything in me to not interact with her, but without an active listener, the thrill was gone. She lost her audience. Did she quit complaining? No. She just found someone else who was willing to listen. But me? I found peace.

QUESTIONS TO PONDER

✦ How can someone be destroyed by having the wrong self-image, perception, or identity? If you have experienced a time when your identity suffered from the opinions of man, how did you overcome?

✦ What does it mean to be a new creation or created in the image of God? Have you experienced a time when your identity was renewed in Christ?

✦ How can you tell when others do not have hope and confidence in God? What characteristics or mannerisms do they exhibit? How can you tell when your own hope and confidence is not centered in Christ?

✦ Do actions really speak louder than words? How do we know when it is safe to trust others and what they say? Have you experienced a time when you put your trust in someone before they earned it? What happened?

✦ Do you think guarding your soul is more like building a wall, being mistrustful, being cautious, or establishing boundaries? How do you guard your soul?

✦ Can having the favor of God also give you the favor of
   man? Have you experienced a time when you stood up
   for your Christian standards in the midst of apparent
   opposition? What happened? Did you win the favor of
   God or man or both?

Jesus told us we should love our neighbor as we love our self
(Mark 12:33). If you have little love and regard for yourself,
however, you won't have much to give out to anyone else. The
point is this: Loving, respecting, and esteeming yourself is not a
selfish act, even though it may seem like one at first. As you make
loving yourself a priority, not only will you strengthen your own
identity, but the quality of love and respect will overflow into
your relationships as well. The practice of forgiveness works in a
similar way. As we embrace forgiveness, not only does our soul
prosper, but our relationships improve as well. Next, we'll look
at how to release the hurts in our life so even more healing can
come.

–9–

STEP NUMBER 2:
Forgiveness

FORGIVENESS: THE PRACTICE OF RIDDING
MY SOUL OF TOXIC WASTE BY CHOOSING TO GIVE UP
JUDGMENTS AGAINST OTHERS.

HAVE YOU EVER BEEN SO ANGRY at someone that you didn't think they deserved a chance to repent? Have you secretly wished God would send calamity and wipe them off the face of the earth? Jonah did. He was a prophet and preacher, but he was bitter. What we commonly refer to as unforgiveness the Bible calls bitterness and it literally means poison. Despite the physical effects bitterness has on our body, it is also deceptive to the point that we often don't recognize our bitterness.

The book of Jonah records Jonah's anger issues and his resulting adventures on the great sea. The drama opens with God calling Jonah to go to the city of Nineveh and preach a message of repentance to the people there. Instead, Jonah bought a ticket on a ship headed in the opposite direction—to Tarshish. Jonah felt justified and ran away from God. He didn't think the people of Ninevah deserved a chance to repent and receive God's forgiveness for their rebellion. Like an angry kid slinging a backpack over his shoulder to leave home, Jonah refused to listen to God's instruction.

God loved the people of Nineveh despite their rebellion. Nineveh was an entire city He wanted to spare. When Jonah refused to listen to His voice, God chose to use circumstances to get his attention. After Jonah set sail for Tarshish, Jonah 1:4 says that God sent a great wind on the sea. But guess what? Jonah was asleep in the boat. The devil will let you sleep in your mess. He'll blind you with false security and make you think you can escape the crisis.

The sailors onboard were afraid for their lives so the captain went scrambling below deck to wake Jonah up. "Hey, buddy, wake up! How can you sleep through this storm? We're all going to die! Please, please, call on your God. Maybe He'll take notice and we will not perish!"

Don't you know when we're making a mess of our life, it affects those around us? And they will literally beg us to do something about it. We may be sleeping through our issues, but we're causing chaos and turmoil to those we sail through life with.

Jonah could have repented at this point, but he didn't. Even a huge storm that threatened the lives of all of the men onboard didn't motivate Jonah to surrender his unforgiveness. He knew he had disobeyed and that the storm was his fault, but he didn't admit it until the crew cast lots and the lot fell on him. "Throw me overboard," Jonah insisted.

> **When we're making a mess of our life, it affects those around us.**

Here's what I find interesting: Jonah was willing to give his life to save these sailors, men he had just met, yet he refused to do the same for the people of Nineveh. It's often easier to forgive someone with whom we don't have history. We aren't emotionally bound to them. That's why so many women jump from one bad relationship straight into the arms of another guy. The new sailor seems perfect. His apparent lack of relationship baggage is an illusion. He's just as whacked out as the last loser, but his issues haven't surfaced yet.

When the storm didn't change Jonah's mind, God used more severe circumstances. Verse seven says that the Lord provided a great fish to swallow him. Other versions say the Lord sent the fish, or the Lord arranged for the fish to swallow Jonah, but I love how the King James Version puts it: "The Lord *prepared* a great fish" (see Jonah 1:17, emphasis added). This fish wasn't filleted, seasoned, and grilled on the BBQ. It wasn't prepared for Jonah's evening meal. In fact, Jonah *was* the meal. The word *prepared* comes from the Hebrew word *manah,* which means to appoint, reckon, ordain, or assign. Jonah had failed his first assignment, and God was merely allowing a retake. Why the drastic measures? Because of Jonah's stubbornness. Jonah hated the people of Nineveh.

> **Sometimes, our issues, chaos, and crises are part of God's plan.**

Sometimes, our issues, chaos, and crises are part of God's plan. Scripture makes clear the fish was not the devil's doing. *God* prepared the fish. Too often we blame the devil on things that God has orchestrated to get our attention and bring us back on track. We'll even try to sleep through the whole mess while everyone around us is screaming for mercy. We can rebuke and curse the circumstances all we want. They'll only get worse. A simple divine request that we try to ignore becomes a raging storm and progresses into a stinky ride in a whale's belly. When we disobey God and try to run away with our bitterness, our issues get nasty and larger than life.

Not all storms are prepared by God, but when we harbor unforgiveness, there's a strong chance that God may do something big to get our attention. How do we know when our storms are divinely orchestrated? The following are four clues that may indicate God is allowing adversity.

YOU'RE RESENTFUL

Is there someone you haven't forgiven? Even after Jonah obeyed God and went to Nineveh, the story ends with Jonah dwelling in bitterness. In chapter four, after he preached a message of repentance to the city of Nineveh and the people obeyed, he traveled outside the city and built a shelter. He wanted to see what would happen to the people of Nineveh. He wanted to witness God's punishment.

When God relented and showed mercy, Jonah was mad. Then he played the classic game of "I told you so."

"I *knew* you were a compassionate God. That's why I was so quick to run to Tarshish" (Jonah 4:2). He was so angry he told God, "I am angry enough to die" (Jonah 4:3).

Have you ever been angry enough to die? Do you resent God's mercy on your ex-husband or previous boyfriend? A small seed of resentment can grow into a huge root of bitterness. Jonah never learned this lesson. He endured a three-day ride in the whale's belly and was vomited ashore, but he never surrendered his anger.

YOU'RE SELF-RIGHTEOUS

Have you ever seen a child comply with his parent's request, but cop an attitude and stomp off afterward? That kind of attitude doesn't please a parent. Nor did Jonah's attitude please God.

It may have looked like Jonah was fully surrendered to God. His actions gave the impression of surrender. On the outside the prophet appeared white-washed and clean, but on the inside, his soul was corrupt. As soon as he opened his mouth, his complaints exposed his bitterness, as if to say, "Look, I did what you wanted, Lord, but I'm not the least bit happy about it."

Jonah may have obeyed God's directive, but he didn't control his soul. Self-righteousness makes the stench of seaweed and whale vomit impossible to remove.

YOU'RE RUNNING FROM GOD

The farther we run away from Him, the more God pursues us. When God called Jonah to go to Ninevah, he ran in the other direction. Because of his stubbornness, it took a lot to get his attention. Even after he acknowledged to the sailors that the tempest was his fault, he still didn't surrender. It wasn't until he spent time in the whale's belly that he cried out to God.

I would think Jonah's cue to cry out to God would have been the threat of being thrown overboard, but Jonah's stubborn heart caused him to underestimate the severity of the sea. Maybe he thought he was an Olympic swimmer. Whatever the case, Jonah thought he could still maneuver out of his mess. He didn't turn to the Lord until he had nowhere else to go. Chapter 2, verse 7 says, "When my life was ebbing away I remembered you,

Lord, and my prayer rose to you." Then he finally acknowledges, "Those who cling to worthless idols forfeit the grace that could be theirs."

You could say "those who cling to bitterness forfeit the grace that could be theirs" (Jonah 2:8).

YOU'RE REPEATING AN ISSUE

As bitter as I once was, the grace of God has allowed multiple opportunities for me to learn how to forgive. I'm not saying that the things I was angry about were trivial or unjust or that God causes adversity so He can teach us a lesson. I will, however, say this: God is more interested in our personal growth than our personal comfort. One way to recognize that God is trying to work on forgiveness in us is when we repeatedly go through the same issues over and over.

Does your issue seem like it's revolving on a merry-go-round? Is there something God has asked you to do that you've refused? If you've already "been here, done that" at least once before, chances are that your repeated issue is another chance prepared by God for you to get it right.

THE PURPOSE OF A CRISIS

In the Chinese language, the word *crisis* is comprised of two symbols that define its meaning. One symbol means chaos or potential danger and the other means hidden opportunity. A crisis is all about perspective. We choose which perspective to embrace; we choose which direction to take. A crisis is like a fork in the road of life that can lead to a turning point if we choose the right path. The destructive path leads to death; the path of hidden opportunity leads to life.

In the English language, a crisis is defined as "a turning point, a stage in a sequence of events at which the trend of all future events, especially for better or for worse, is determined."[13] Often our crisis is a dramatic emotional and circumstantial upheaval; but through our crisis, God wants to birth something. In the medical field, a health crisis is the point in the course of a serious disease at which a decisive change occurs, leading either to recovery or to death. Similarly, at some point in our crisis, we choose either recovery or despair. When we get to the end of our rope, we need to let go of the rope and grab onto hope.

Kim Clement, teacher and songwriter, explains it like this:

Within every crisis is a hidden opportunity. The word for crisis is the same word used to describe a birthing stool, the seat on which Jewish women sat as they gave birth. So during a crisis, you are giving birth. Out of this pain, you are going to bring forth something great, and it will come from within you. Instead of trying to lay blame, remember that God has given you a promise.

When Joseph was falsely imprisoned, instead of hiding away in misery, he prospered because he believed that he was to take advantage of his circumstances. He knew that he would make it to the promise that God had given him. He prophesied and interpreted dreams while he was in prison. When you find yourself in a crisis, you must function as though you are already living in your promise. In crisis, do what God told you to do, and you will find what is hidden. Our crisis is the birthing ground for unrealized destiny.[14]

After my affairs were discovered, I felt stripped, exposed, and alone. I had no idea how to deal with my emotions without stuffing them or running to another relationship. Hopeless and frightened, I finally hit bottom. I knew I needed more help than Pastor Dan was able to give.

I had attended Al-Anon meetings in the past when Tom went to Alcoholics Anonymous. Al-Anon is a support group for people in relationship with an alcoholic or addict. I couldn't relate to those ladies at all. They talked about things like having peace despite the problems in their relationship and how to focus on themselves instead of trying to change their partner. They talked about boundaries and about how they could only change themselves. At the time, I saw no need to change myself. I wasn't an alcoholic or a drug addict. I was the responsible one. My husband was the one with the problems. I attended meetings for two years without gaining a bit of knowledge. But now I understand a key truth: Those ladies had peace and I didn't. I decided to give the program another try.

It was a Saturday morning meeting in January, and the subject was—yet again—peace. I sat on a metal folding chair in a circle of women I didn't know. One by one, volunteers read an excerpt out of the ODAT (*One Day at a Time*) book. I had heard the same pages read numerous times before, but now, something was different. For the first time, I listened for *me*.

A ray of sunshine streamed in through the window. I watched as dust particles danced in the beam. Then it hit me. Light and dust can coexist. Despite the junk going on around me, I can embrace peace and happiness. My contentment is not attached to someone else's actions. All of a sudden, everything I had previously heard in Al-Anon meetings made sense. It was as if numerous files saved in temporary storage were suddenly downloaded to my heart, and in one instant, truth illuminated my soul. It was one of the most profound awakenings my soul had ever felt.

My desire to change was the key that unlocked my recovery. I also had to acknowledge my issues and take responsibility for my own actions. Finally, I realized my need to change, and my desire matched it. No longer was I focused on trying to change someone else. Thus began my recovery from relationship addiction. Years of denied feelings left me with a lot of unresolved issues, but in the Bible, I found tools to deal with my emotions that I previously didn't even know existed because I had stuffed them so deep inside.

Isaiah 43:18-19 became my life line. "Forget the former things; do not dwell on the past. See! I am doing a new thing. Now it springs up. Do you not perceive it? I am making a way in the desert and streams in the wilderness."

God sent women to help me, encourage me, and pray for me. The first woman was my sponsor in Al-Anon. Ironically, her name was also Christy. She instructed me to call her whenever I needed someone to talk to. She probably didn't know how often that would be. Most of my calls began with a bitter complaint about Tom, like this conversation:

"Tom didn't go to work today even though he promised that he would! I'm crazy mad. I'm so angry I had to leave the house to call you and get away from him. I don't know what to do!"

She replied: "Christy, I'm sorry to hear that. I'm sure you are disappointed, but remember, I'm not Tom's sponsor. I can't change him and neither can you. So let's talk about you. Let's talk about your options. What can you do?"

"I have no clue. I can't make him go to work! Lord knows I've tried and nothing gets through!"

"That's right. You can't make Tom do anything. Christy, in the past, you only saw options that involved changing someone else's behavior. You've tried control tactics, threats, tears and shouts. But the only person you can change is yourself, so let's look at your options."

Light and dust can coexist. Despite the junk going on around me, I can embrace peace and happiness.

"The only options I see are to be angry or let it go, and I'm not about to let it go. I can't accept the fact that he isn't willing to go to work."

"There are more options than what you see."

"I don't understand," I said.

"One thing you might consider is to change your expectations."

More anger well up within me. "You mean lower my expectations? I can't do that! I *expect* my husband to go to work."

"I get that, Christy," my sponsor said. "But let me explain something. If every day you have an expectation that your husband goes to work and 75 percent of the time he sleeps in and stays at home, according to the two options you have given yourself, 75 percent of the time, you are going to be angry. You are in essence giving him rule over your peace."

"But I simply cannot lower my expectations!"

"Actually I didn't suggest that you *lower* your expectations. I suggested that you *change* them. Your expectations, although reasonable, are not realistic. There is a difference between having reasonable and realistic expectations. Yes, it is a reasonable expectation that your husband should go to work and provide for his family, but is it a realistic expectation, given his character and addiction issues?"

I let that sink in. "No, I guess not."

"Could you give yourself another option? Instead of only allowing yourself to be angry or let it go, could you add another option to change your expectation? If you change your expectation to be more realistic, given his history of broken promises, would you agree that you would probably be less angry?"

"Probably so."

"Our expectations are a set-up for disappointment and bitterness. You can't change Tom's actions, but you can change your responses to his actions. If you do, you stand a better chance of walking in peace. Would that be worth it to you?"

How could I argue with that logic? "Yes, it would. I will try," I agreed.

> *Changing my expectations was something I had to do for me so that I could guard my heart and soul from bitterness.*

It was probably the hardest thing I ever did, but changing my expectations was something I had to do for me so that I could guard my heart and soul from bitterness. I also learned to guard my soul by being out of the house in the morning when Tom didn't get up so I wouldn't be tempted to scream at him. Removing myself from the situation that provoked my anger helped me focus on my own reactions. Eventually, I learned to react less and less to his behavior. And eventually, my peace increased.

I wish I could say everything in my life and marriage got better really fast. But it didn't. It's a funny thing about peace. The only way to get true peace is to push past adversity.

Throughout the next several months, I learned many life-changing truths, but most importantly, I finally accepted responsibility to change myself. I had tried for years to change my husband, thinking that he was the problem. All the while, I ignored the fact that if I wanted to be happy, I had to determine to be happy. I spent the next several years of my marriage hoping and praying that my husband would experience recovery as well. God had done so much to restore my life, so I prayed that my husband would surrender his life to God too. I wanted our marriage to be restored. Instead, Tom spiraled further into his drug addiction, adding verbal and emotional abuse to his bag of tricks. After our middle child, Garrett, was born, issues intensified again and we separated for a second time. I prayed and waited. We got back together a year later.

My husband promised changes that only proved to be temporary manipulation tactics to get me back. But despite his verbal abuse and drug addiction, I was healing. I learned that forgiveness facilitates joy. As the burden of bitterness moved out, the more my capacity to receive God's joy moved in. God showed me how to walk in joy despite the conflict around me. It was a long journey out of the wilderness, and through it I learned that happiness depends on things and circumstances, but joy comes from the Lord.

By the time Tom and I divorced eight years later, I was not the same person. A surrendered life and years of adversity had transformed my life into something brand new. I liked my new life. I despised my old one. Although there were several invitations to go back, I didn't want to return to my prison of bitterness. Misery loves company, and bitterness was still familiar. The pull back to the wilderness where I spent so much of my life was like a magnetic field. That's why so many people go back to addictions after a measure of recovery. It takes work to stay free. We have to change bad habits, make wise choices, and hang around wisdom.

Two years after our divorce, Tom had our two boys, Garrett and Jake, for his weekend visitation. By this time, he had a decent job and I thought he was rebuilding his life. I had no idea he had returned to his addiction again. On Saturday morning, June 13, 1998, he made plans to go to his brother's house to take the boys fishing with his brother and nephew Cody. It was Cody's thirteenth birthday, but Tom never made it to their house. Driving under the influence of Methadone, Demerol, Xanax, Valium, and Benadryl, Tom hit another car head-on at 10:00 in the morning. Our youngest son, Jake, died at the scene. Garrett spent five days in Children's Hospital with a fractured jaw.

There are no words to describe the agony of losing a child. I had every right to be angry. I had every right to fall back into despair.

I once heard someone say that when we don't want to forgive, we can pray for willingness. Sometimes, even asking for willingness can be difficult, but God will deliver it. Once we are willing and choose to forgive, an amazing thing happens. The grace to walk in forgiveness comes. It did for me. There is no way I was strong enough to forgive on my own, but I didn't want to go back to my former life. If I learned one thing from years of taming my sin of bitterness, it was that unforgiveness was a deadly disease that would take me straight back to bondage. If I allowed bitterness to contaminate my soul once again, I knew I would die in my misery. Oh, it wouldn't have been an immediate death. The leprosy of bitterness is more deceptive than that. At first, I may not even notice it because it was so familiar. Mine would have been a slow death with the grasp of bitterness growing tighter with each passing day.

If I allowed bitterness to contaminate my soul once again, I knew I would die in my misery.

For years, I clung to Isaiah 43:18-19. These Scriptures again became my lifeline. I couldn't afford to look back. I had walked daily trusting God with hurts, insults, false accusations, and disappointments. And now, my only hope was to trust Him again. Nothing was going to bring Jake back. Resentment would only bury me in anger again. I didn't *feel* like forgiving, but the alternative of resentment was no longer a suitable choice.

As I chose to forgive, an incredible thing happened. God began to fill me with joy in the midst of my pain. I had never felt such a powerful force of joy in my life, and it made no sense that I could experience joy in the midst of such tragedy. Yet somehow, I was keenly aware that the joy was more than I was capable of containing. The joy was to be shared; the only way I could keep it was to give it away. My destiny changed the day Jake died. The purpose for his life was transfused into mine.

In the movie, *The Guardian*, Randall, the only survivor of a deadly mission, was advised of an opening for an instructor position. The last thing he wanted to do was teach. But his superior sternly advised him, "I need you to train the next generation." Struggling with the loss of his crewmembers, he threw himself into his newest assignment. The birth of Randall's purpose originated out of a great tragedy. His motto ultimately became, "So Others May Live." The byline of the movie asserts that "your darkest hour can be your finest moment."

Along similar lines, my hope is sustained by memorializing Jake's life. For me, it's not optional. It's necessary to maintain my joy. Proverbs 10:7 says, "The memory of the righteous shall be a blessing." Since the accident, I determined to carry the celebration of his life beyond the funeral. I may have buried my son, but I did not bury his future or his purpose. His future and purpose did not die with his physical death because the kingdom of God does not operate with the same principles as the world.

Death does not mean finality. Eternity embraces our past, present, *and* future. Jake left a legacy of hope and joy in the midst of the storm. It is now my purpose to train other women to acquire the vision to see beyond life's difficulties. That is my mandate from heaven. Whether I initially wanted that assignment or not, my "Superior" advised me that He needed me to train the next generation. That is the purpose I was created for, the mission that keeps me awake at night, and the calling I was born to complete.

Out of our greatest pain often comes our greatest change—a birth of something greater, a birth of purpose and destiny. What pain, bitterness, or unforgiveness are you dealing with right now?

In the midst of your pain, God is building something in you. Let Him complete His work. Don't go through the agony and leave the victory behind. You must have forgiveness in order for Him to build you up, so do everything you can to overlook an offense. Perhaps that sounds simplistic in theory, but you can forgive and be free from bitterness.

-10-

Forgive AND Forget?

"I MAY BE CHANGED BY WHAT HAPPENS TO ME,
BUT I REFUSE TO BE REDUCED BY IT."
—MAYA ANGELOU

DID YOU KNOW BITTERNESS is a poison? It not only affects our emotions, but left untreated, the toxins produced by bitterness eventually seep into our body as well. Resentment can cause all kinds of physical ailments.

In her book *Who Switched Off My Brain?* Dr. Caroline Leaf reports, "A massive body of research shows that up to 80 percent of physical, emotional, and mental health issues today could be a direct result of our thought lives. Resentment, bitterness, lack of forgiveness and self-hatred are just a few of the toxic thoughts and emotions that can also trigger immune system disorders."[15]

The grasp of bitterness is deceptive. Have you ever hung onto a grudge because you wanted to punish the other person only to notice that you are the only one suffering? Even when we know how destructive bitterness can be, it is difficult to release because it goes against our sin nature. We want to be in charge. We want to dole out the consequences. We become like an angry rattlesnake. If infuriated and threatened enough, a rattlesnake will bite itself and die from its own poison. Likewise, our own anger is self-inflicted venom. We may not literally die, but we feel dead. We become the walking wounded.

No matter how much we want vengeance, Deuteronomy 29:18 warns us, "Make sure there is no root among you that produces such bitter poison." Just like the habit of hanging onto resentment, releasing forgiveness is a decision and reaction. It's a choice. And the more we practice forgiveness, the easier it becomes to tear down the walls of bitterness.

> *The more we practice forgiveness, the easier it becomes to tear down the walls of bitterness.*

How many times have you heard someone say, "I'll forgive, but I'll never forget!"? In *The Message,* Proverbs 19:11 says, "Smart people know how to hold their tongue; their grandeur is to forgive and forget." Since most of us equate forgetting with having no memory or recollection of an offense, this directive is difficult to understand. God can do anything. He can forget whatever He wants, but what about us humans? What exactly does it mean to forgive and forget? Is it possible to erase our minds? If we remember the offense, does that mean we haven't forgiven? To comprehend this mystery, let's examine what the Bible means when it says that God doesn't remember our sins.

Isaiah 43:25 says, "I, even I, am the one who wipes out your transgressions for My own sake; and I will not remember your sins." The word *remember* used in this verse comes from the Hebrew word *zakar,* which means to recall, to mention, call to mind, to record, or to make a memorial.

Here's the key: When God says He will not remember our sins, it means He will not recall them, mention them, call them to mind, record them, or make a memorial. We tend to equate forgetting with "not remembering." And it doesn't make sense because we can't possibly forget something that happened, can we?

Maybe this will bring relief. Forgetting doesn't mean we've lost the memory—it means we've lost the emotional charge related to the memory. We no longer hold our offender responsible to pay up. We've discontinued punishment and released them from penance. All penalties have been removed.

But how often do we "forgive" and bring the matter up again? Or how often do we make a memorial out of our pain? It's been said that misery loves company. So does bitterness. Some people enjoy the attention their misery brings. Their bitterness is a love/hate relationship that becomes a constant companion and an addictive, consuming trap. Most often their propensity to remain bitter is due to false beliefs about forgiveness. So let's go over a few points about forgiveness.

+ Forgiveness is a choice.

+ Forgiveness doesn't mean the other person's actions were acceptable.

+ Forgiving others doesn't release them from the natural consequences of their actions or legal obligation for restitution.

+ Forgiveness does not always lead to reconciliation.

+ Forgiving is not something we do for the other person.

✦ We forgive out of obedience to God.

✦ We forgive so that the chains of bitterness don't destroy our soul-health.

✦ It only takes one person to forgive.

✦ Forgiveness is an access to great joy.

✦ Forgiving someone doesn't mean you have to trust the offender again.

✦ Forgiveness is required, but trust has to be earned.

In the Bible, Joseph exemplifies someone who was able to forgive and forget. After being sold into human trafficking by his jealous brothers, being falsely accused of rape, and being thrown in prison, Joseph easily could have justified his anger and bitterness. His brother's actions were clearly wrong, but he overlooked their offense. In a gripping encounter twenty-two years later, Joseph said to the brothers who sold him into slavery, "You intended to harm me, but God intended it for good to accomplish what is now being done, the saving of many lives" (Genesis 50:20).

Joseph was someone who learned how to forgive *and* forget. He refused to throw the matter up again in the faces of his offenders. He still "recalled" the event. It wasn't somehow magically erased from his memory, but Joseph didn't use the memory to file additional charges against his offenders. He was past the pain. The emotional charge was gone and the obligation to repay the debt was erased.

How can you tell if you're past your pain? Here are some ways you can tell if you've forgiven and forgotten.

- The "tapes" are erased. You no longer replay mental conversations.

- You can pray for the person who offended you.

- You don't feel anxious when you see them.

- You don't secretly rejoice if you hear of problems they suffer.

- You can feel compassion for them.

- You can be genuinely kind when you see them.

- You have peace when you think of them.

- You have no more expectations of the person who offended you.

You can move past your pain. If Joseph did it, so can you! I want to challenge you to release your expectations. The more you do, the less offense you will endure. The ultimate goal would be to deny the offense in the first place because expectations are a down payment on resentment.

To help you strengthen your ability to forgive, the next chapter lists several Scriptures on forgiveness. Find a few that speak to you and ask the Lord to bring you revelation and show you people you need to forgive. (You may also consider whether there are any organizations, employers or even churches or ministries that you need to forgive.) Then look over the list of action points and select a few you think will help you on your forgiveness journey. For additional study, consider the questions to ponder. I'm praying for you as you dive into God's Word and allow Him to do a soul detox!

—11—

Strengthening Forgiveness

WHEN JOSEPH WAS SEVENTEEN, he had a dream that he and his brothers were binding sheaves of grain, when suddenly his sheaf rose up and the others gathered around his and bowed down (Genesis 37:7). Perhaps God gave Joseph the dream to fuel his ability to endure years of family rejection, slavery, and false imprisonment. The vision served as a focal point that enabled Joseph to press past the adversity because he knew there was a promise on the other side of the pain. The dream was a glimpse of the final product, but Joseph still had to choose where he would fix his eyes.

There is a biblical route to divine destiny. The roadmap to our destiny starts out with a dream. Often there is a desert between the dream and our destiny. Even though we didn't sign up for it, the desert is where we grow in Christ. God uses the adversity of our wilderness experience to perfect us and transform us into His image.

While we are in the desert, we get to choose where we go next. The intended destination is our destiny, but if we don't forgive those who hurt us, we run the risk of wandering in the desert much longer than we might otherwise. The Israelites wandered for forty years. Their complaining and murmuring prevented them access to their promise. Unfortunately, they died in their misery without ever laying eyes on the promise of God.

Has God planted a dream in your heart? If so, you probably have spent some time in the desert. Maybe it feels like you'll never escape. Keep believing. Fix your eyes on the promise. Choose to forgive. One day, God will produce your destiny.

Joseph was a master at forgiveness. He knew how to rid his soul of toxic waste by choosing to give up judgments against others. I pray the following Scriptures, action points, and questions to ponder will help you on your forgiveness journey.

FORGIVENESS SCRIPTURE TRUTHS

- ✦ "See to it that no one misses the grace of God and that no bitter root grows up to cause trouble and defile many" (Hebrews 12:15).

- ✦ "A person's wisdom yields patience; it is to one's glory to overlook an offense" (Proverbs 19:11).

- ✦ "Whoever would foster love covers over an offense, but whoever repeats the matter separates close friends" (Proverbs 17:9).

- ✦ "In your anger do not sin. Do not let the sun go down while you are still angry, and do not give the devil a foothold" (Ephesians 4:26-27).

✦ "For I see that you are full of bitterness and captive to sin" (Acts 8:23).

✦ "Opponents must be gently instructed, in the hope that God will grant them repentance leading to a knowledge of the truth, and that they will come to their senses and escape from the trap of the devil, who has taken them captive to do his will" (2 Timothy 2:25-26).

✦ "If we confess our sins, he is faithful and just and will forgive us our sins and purify us from all unrighteousness" (1 John 1:9).

✦ "He who conceals his sins does not prosper, but whoever confesses and renounces them finds mercy" (Proverbs 28:13).

✦ "Make sure there is no man or woman, clan or tribe among you today whose heart turns away from the LORD our God to go and worship the gods of those nations; make sure there is no root among you that produces such bitter poison" (Deuteronomy 29:18).

✦ "Do not make friends with a hot-tempered man, do not associate with one easily angered, or you may learn his ways, and get yourself ensnared" (Proverbs 22:24-25).

✦ "This is how my heavenly Father will treat each of you unless you forgive your brother from your heart" (Matthew 18:35).

+ "And when you stand praying, if you hold anything against anyone, forgive them, so that your Father in heaven may forgive you your sins" (Mark 11:25).

FORGIVENESS ACTION POINTS

Remember, forgiveness is the practice of cleansing our soul of toxic waste by choosing to give up judgments against others. If you are ready for cleansing your soul, try these action points:

Manage Your Expectations

My friend John told me about his rebound marriage after his seventeen-year first marriage ended. "Honestly, it's been harder for me to deal with the aftershock from my short marriage," he said. "I'm drawn to needy women, and I didn't realize it at first, but my second wife is mentally ill. It makes no sense that I'm angry at the things she does. She literally can't help it. Even so, bitterness literally consumes me. I know I shouldn't be angry, but I can't forgive. It's like being mad at a toddler for not being able to do math."

Expectations are a set-up for disappointment and bitterness. There's a difference between reasonable and realistic expectations. When we expect others to behave reasonably, especially those who are incapable, our expectations are unrealistic. Disappointment is the inevitable result. If we don't deal with disappointment, bitterness sets in.

Teresa was married to an alcoholic. Despite the obvious problems she endured in her relationship, she was one of the most peaceful women I knew. "It's *reasonable* that I would expect my husband to be sober when I get home from work," she explained to me one day. "But until Jerry is willing to go to treatment, it's not *realistic* for me to expect him to be without a drink in his hand. I spent years expecting otherwise and I was always angry. I'd rather live in peace."

When you manage your expectations, you avoid the pitfall of unforgiveness and increase your peace of mind.

Guard Your Heart

I have a secret weapon for walking in peace and forgiveness. If you implement this one Scripture, you're almost guaranteed to eliminate at least half of the issues you ever deal with. Proverbs 4:23 says, "Guard your heart for out of it flow the issues of life."

Before I understood this verse, I was a "yes" woman. I thought saying yes to everything was the spiritual thing to do, so I did everything everyone wanted me to do, even when it made me angry. It took a long time before I figured out that if doing something makes me angry, I had no business doing it.

The Bible refers to setting boundaries as guarding your heart. Did you notice who is responsible for putting the guard in place? We are! If saying "yes" results in bitterness, it was wrong for you. Learn to say "no" to guard your heart.

When you guard your heart, you protect yourself against toxic emotions. It's like buying an insurance policy against bitterness. Guarding your heart and setting boundaries can help you avoid the trap of bitterness more than any other anger-management technique.

Identify areas in your life that trigger your anger and then put guards in place to protect those areas. Be cautious around people who trigger your anger. Avoid them if possible. Anger in itself is not a sin, but unresolved anger that turns into bitterness is sin.

Get Your Mind Off the Offense

Your countenance is the product of what you think about most often. So if you don't want to be angry, refuse to meditate on angry thoughts. You can't just empty your mind, however. You have to occupy the void. Choose the emotional response you desire and select a thought or activity that will produce that outcome. Eventually, since you can't maintain more than one emotion at a time, whatever you feed begins to grow and whatever you starve begins to die.

When Shirley's husband slept in on Sundays, she often went to church angry. "By the time I got home, I had nursed my grudge for two hours, and it showed. It made Ronnie even more determined to avoid church the following week. Now I understand why he didn't want to go to church with me—I was always angry."

Instead of focusing on her disappointment when her husband slept in, Shirley began to focus on positive things about her husband. Ronnie usually had Sunday lunch ready when she got home, so Shirley began to meditate about how happy that made her. When she got home her husband was surprised. He was used to the angry countenance Shirley wore. Instead, she was genuinely grateful and happy to see him. Not only did Shirley learn how to get her mind off the offense, eventually Ronnie quit sleeping in on Sundays.

Pray for God to Bless

Feelings follow actions, so even when it doesn't feel genuine to pray for someone you are angry with, do it anyway. Fake it till you make it. Do it until you aren't angry anymore. The Bible says to bless your enemies. As you do, something amazing begins to happen: The more you pray for them the more your anger will subside.

Pick an Attribute You Admire

Often when we're angry with someone, there is an emotional barrier that prevents us from seeing any good in them. Our bitterness camouflages reality. This is when you may need to reach into the recesses of your memory. What did you like or enjoy about them before? If you can't come up with anything, ask God to help you see something good. Then focus on that. People respond to our expectations of them and often their behavior will rise and fall based on how we treat them. If you are angry and unkind to them, chances are great that you will get angry and unkind responses back from them. Smother them with kindness and watch your own anger dissolve.

Make a Gratitude List

Create a list of things you are grateful for and spend five minutes each morning renewing your mind and meditating on God's goodness. Carry your list with you so when you are tempted to think on things that weigh your spirit down you can quickly lift your spirit by remembering God's goodness.

Overlook an Offense

Holding on to bitterness is like holding a glass of water above your head. At first it doesn't seem heavy. You can hold it for a minute with no problem. After an hour, your arm might ache. And after a day, you'll need a crane to help you hold up a mere glass of water. It all depends on how long you hold it. The longer you hold it, the heavier it gets.

Overlooking an offense before it weighs a ton is much easier. Choose to overlook a transgression to protect your own sanity. Do it before you carry it so long that the burden becomes an unmanageable monster.

Change Your Meditations

Stop the negative self-talk. Don't give anyone free rent space in your head.

In her book *Having a Mary Spirit*, Joanna Weaver writes about muscle memory, which "refers to the experience when muscles seem to perform almost automatically without conscious thought. It's a physical pattern developed by many years of practice."[16]

For most of us, our brains have developed thinking patterns and have years of experience of routing our thoughts along certain neural pathways. We've worn grooves in our brain. It will take deliberate conscious thought to reroute our thinking. It won't happen overnight, but it can happen if we purpose in our heart what we allow ourselves to think about. We become what we most think about. If we think angry thoughts, we will be angry. If we think happy thoughts, we become happy. Abraham Lincoln said it best: "Most folks are as happy as they make up their minds to be." We could also reword that to say most people are as angry as they make up their minds to be.

Pray for Revelation

When I speak to singles groups, the question I hear more than any other is, "How did you know John was the one?"

Before I met my second husband, John, like most other singles, I had my "list." I knew what I wanted. I wanted someone older, sophisticated and well established, and although John was nice, he didn't have any of those qualities. He was younger, goofy, and still in college—the exact opposite of what I was looking for. Left to my own romantic discernment, I wouldn't have picked John. But thank goodness, God knew my picker was busted.

It was a Wednesday evening after work on January 28, 1998. John had driven up from Lawton, Oklahoma, for dinner after his classes. With three small children, going out to eat was a rare occurrence. After dessert, we plopped down on the worn blue sofa in my TV room and John asked, "Do you mind if I pray?" To this day, I don't even remember what his prayer was about, but what happened next, I'll never forget ...

An overwhelming presence of peace engulfed me, and I felt my heart—not my physical heart, but the heart of my soul—being knit together with John's. I know it sounds cheesy, but it's the only way I can describe the supernatural experience that took place. I say "supernatural" because in the natural, I wouldn't have picked John. He wasn't my type.

But here's the deal: I never had much success in the relation-ship department. God knew that without a divine revelation I would go back to devastation.

The next morning I marched into the office and announced to my coworker Julie, "I'm going to marry John." He hadn't even proposed yet, but I *knew*. John was God's pick, not Christy's pick. I knew John was a divine connection, a heavenly match—not just a good choice, but a God choice. Later when conflicts arose in our relationship, it was this revelation that brought back peace.

If you ask God for revelation, He will reveal His plans for you, too.

Seek Advice

Before we got married, I thought John was perfect. We'll never argue, I thought. The bliss of love kept me smothered in romantic ignorance.

Until we got married.

It was only a couple of months before our first major blowout. As a couple, we had much to learn about effective conflict resolution. My preferred method of resolving disagreements was to attack and blame—a full frontal assault with lethal accusations.

He preferred to run.

When John started packing his suitcase, anger steamed in me until it spewed out like hot lava. John had ignited Mount St. Christy. *How could I trust him again?* I seethed. But when the volcanic ash settled down, I remembered the revelation that my soul was knit together with John's.

Conviction washed over me.

Of course, that wasn't the last time we got into a disagreement, but I don't want to be a statistic. In our culture, the option of divorce is an easy escape. According to Jennifer Baker of The Forest Institute of Professional Psychology in Springfield, Missouri, the divorce rate in America for first marriages is 50 percent and jumps to 67 percent for second marriages and 74 percent for third marriages.[17] Why so high? When conflict comes, many run. They think they made a mistake, but conflict is a natural part of life. Conflict is the mechanism that God often uses to strengthen our character and endurance.

I thank God for my marriage mentor. She listened to me vent, but wasn't afraid of letting me know when I was wrong. "It doesn't matter who is right or wrong. You are one flesh," Alicia encouraged. "Proverbs 12:16 says, 'it's to a man's glory to overlook an offense.'"

Eventually, I thought I had matured to the point where I was able to control my anger. I prided myself on my ability to restrain my temper and sarcasm. The volcano was dormant, but it was still brewing on the inside. Once again Alicia pointed me to the Scriptures. Proverbs 25:28 says, "He that hath no rule over his own spirit is like a city that is broken down, and without walls" (KJV).

Now when offenses come, I ask the Lord, "What are you trying to work out in me through this conflict?"

We all have blind spots in our lives, dangerous habits that are obvious to others but we can't see. I never would have seen this truth without the insight of a trusted friend and mentor. We all need at least one friend that we can trust to be confidential as well as to tell it like it is.

QUESTIONS TO PONDER

How do you think Joseph came to his point of forgiveness? Do you think he would have been used by God to save the world from famine if he remained in bitterness?

+ Why is it so important to let go of bitterness before we go to bed?

+ How can bitterness grow and hold us captive to sin?

+ How does confessing our sins give us freedom?

+ Have you personally experienced liberty after a season of trying to hide your struggles? What happened?

+ Like a small root that grows into a great tree, bitterness springs up in our hearts and overshadows even our deepest Christian relationships. A bitter root comes when we allow disappointment to grow into resentment or when we nurse grudges over past hurts. What other unhealthy emotions usually accompany bitterness?

+ How do you know if someone has issues with anger?

+ Is bitterness contagious? Have you seen a group of people plagued by the bitterness of one person? Have you experienced the bitterness of others? How did you deal with the situation?

+ Forgiveness often feels like something we do for the person who offended us, but harboring bitterness blocks our ability to receive forgiveness. Why is God more concerned about our freedom than defending our cause and proving us right? Have you ever experienced a dramatic release after a long period of holding onto bitterness?

Forgiveness is one of the most difficult of the seven steps to breaking the toxic love cycle, but also one of the most healing. Once you've cleansed your soul of bitterness, you are well on your way to becoming soul-healthy. Just remember to continue to examine yourself when offenses threaten to steal your peace. We wash laundry every week because our clothing gets soiled and stinky. Why not wash the stain and stench of offense out of our soul? Nothing smells better than fresh laundry! So inhale deeply and get ready. Next we'll learn how to look at our circumstances from God's perspective as we dive into the third step to breaking the toxic love cycle: Embracing the habit of imagination.

−12−

STEP NUMBER 3:
Imagination

IMAGINATION: The practice of maintaining
a healthy thought life so I can follow
God's vision for my future.

WHEN I WAS MARRIED to my first husband, I often called my Al-Anon sponsor for advice, first giving a detailed account of the horrible things my husband did to me. One day I cried out, "Why won't he cherish me?"

"Look up 2 Corinthians 10:5," Christy said. "And memorize it."

I knew better than to argue with my sponsor. Not only did she know the Bible, she lived with a raging alcoholic and yet she was one of the most content women I knew. I flipped open my Bible and read the verse silently: "We demolish arguments and every pretension that sets itself up against the knowledge of God, and we take captive every thought to make it obedient to Christ."

I sighed. "You'll have to interpret this for me. I have *no* idea what this means. I just want him to love me."

"Christy, you've got this backward. If you want him to cherish you, *you* have to cherish you. The way others see you is a reflection of how you see yourself. If you want others to see you differently, *you* have to imagine yourself differently."

As I learned to apply truth from the Word of God to my injured soul, I found myself shielded from my husband's insults. I relied more on what God said about me and less on Tom's accusations. I learned that what others say about me is not nearly as important as what I say about myself or what God says about me. Before I learned how powerful the gift of our imagination is, I thought exercising my imagination was a futile exercise—something dreamers do—and a pointless escape to a fantasy land. But today I see evidence in Scripture to support the use of imagination. As long as what I imagine agrees with God's truth, the outcome can only be beneficial. What is the other option? If I agreed with my husband's insults, his words would define me.

The book of Matthew acknowledges this truth: "Whenever two or more on earth agree, so shall it be" (18:19). I've always quoted this Scripture to "seal the deal" on prayer requests, but even when we agree with careless words, the "two-or-more, so-shall-it-be" clause still applies. Then the inevitable happens. The repeated lies of the enemy become deeply embedded doubts that are difficult to erase.

Consider this Proverb, which I paraphrase: "As a *woman* thinks in her heart, so shall *she* be" (23:7). When insults surround you, remember—your imagination is a powerful resource. You are created in the image of God (Genesis 1:27) and He cherishes you. You are the apple of His eye (Zechariah 2:8), and He rejoices over you with singing (Zephaniah 3:17). Choose to agree with God's Word and bring your imagination into alignment to His truth. As you do, an incredible thing happens. Not only will you feel better about yourself, but others will begin to treat you differently as well. What you believe about yourself is contagious. How you perceive yourself predicts how others will treat you.

GUARD AGAINST DISCOURAGEMENT

Once we embrace *the truth*, we must guard ourselves against discouragement. In the book of Exodus, we read that God led the children of Israel out of the bondage of Egypt through one miracle after another. He had an itinerary for His people. Their intended destination was the Promised Land, a land flowing with milk and honey. But they never saw it. Instead, those that wandered in the desert *died* in the desert. Why? Because they allowed discouragement to overwhelm them. Their discouragement caused them to forfeit their inheritance.

> *How you perceive yourself predicts how others will treat you.*

God did not want the next generation to make the same mistake. After the death of Moses, God chose Joshua to lead the next generation. In Joshua 1:9, He instructed Joshua firmly, "Have I not commanded you? Be strong and courageous! Do not be afraid or discouraged." Discouragement thwarts the purpose of God. When we are discouraged, God's plan for our life is hindered. We will be defeated until we deliberately replace our discouraging thoughts.

Why replace discouragement rather than eliminate it? Because our mind is constantly active and we can't get rid of thoughts. We can only replace them. But we can *choose* which thoughts we allow access. Discouragement is the result of toxic thoughts we allow ourselves to entertain. Likewise, encouragement is the result of thinking encouraging thoughts.

Replacing our thoughts takes a lot of work. A number of years ago the National Science Foundation estimated that our brains produce as many as 50,000 thoughts per day. While the majority of them are the same as the day before, many experts agree that about two-thirds of them are negative thoughts. If we want to change our thoughts and eliminate negative repeat offenders, it will require discipline, focus, and determination. When a police officer is planning an arrest to take an offender captive, she has to plan a strategy for the stakeout. Once she apprehends the offender, she has to handcuff him and lock him up. A lot of force is involved. It's a hostile situation. In the same way, it requires force to apprehend our thoughts.

An example that best illustrates my point occurred during an interview with Tyler Perry before the release of his movie *Why Did I Get Married?* Prior to his success in the film industry, Tyler Perry spent years being homeless. A reporter questioning Mr. Perry about his years of poverty and his rise to film success asked him this question:

"With all that is happening to you now—when you were growing up in New Orleans, did you ever imagine that you would be in this position?"

"Yes, I did imagine!" was Tyler Perry's reply.

The reporter was shocked. He said, "You don't think that's a little arrogant?"

Perry's answer was bold. "I *had* to imagine myself in a better place. Sometimes the nights got so cold and the days so hard and long that if I hadn't, I wouldn't have made it."

Likewise ladies, we cannot achieve victory unless we first imagine it.

In an email advising of his interview, Mr. Perry encouraged his viewers, "When you think about your tomorrow, are good things waiting for you? When you imagine your future, are you happy and blessed? Is your family happy? Are you in a better place than you are now? If you don't see good things in your future then nothing good will come your way."

Well put, Tyler Perry.

God wants us to imagine truths that produce victory for our situations. We need to see the victory in our spirit before it manifests. When we mentally imagine and envision our future, we have a champion mentality.

You may think that sounds hard, but ladies, we do it all the time with wordly pursuits. Many of us use a different name for it—fantasizing. We all know how to do that. Not all fantasy is wrong, but the enemy definitely has a counterfeit for everything God creates. Our imaginations may only be ungodly fantasies when they are inspired by our flesh, but when they are birthed by God, He commands us to meditate on the dream He has put in our heart. Without the dream, we will be void of vision, and without vision, we will never achieve victory.

Recall the passage I quoted earlier: "Forget the former things; do not dwell on the past. See, I am doing a new thing! Now it springs up; do you not perceive it? I am making a way in the desert and streams in the wasteland" (Isaiah 43:18-19).

When God is getting ready to do a new thing, He wants us to acquire the ability to perceive. He wants us to see the newness before it actually manifests. And most importantly, He wants us to discard the former things and forget about the past. Looking behind does not help us move forward.

VISUALIZING VICTORY

We will end up at the place where we fix our gaze. Until we acquire God's vision, our own vision will cause disappointment. Failure to press through only gets us another trip around the wilderness.

Carving a new trail is hard at first. It takes determination and willpower to guard against discouragement. Why is it so wrong to walk in discouragement? Because discouragement turns into self-pity and bitterness. We can't stand against fear if we are discouraged. We'll end up losing our vision and become disillusioned. When we turn our gaze away from the vision and direction in which we are headed, we will surely stumble.

> *Without a dream, we will be void of vision, and without vision, we will never achieve victory.*

When we drive our vehicle, we keep our gaze fixed ahead. We only glance over our shoulder or check our rear view mirror to make sure our path is clear when we turn or change lanes. None of us would drive by only looking into our side mirror or rear view mirrors. These are intended to help us avoid collision. It's the same with keeping our gaze on God. If we fix our eyes on Him, we will get to our intended destination, but if a glance in another direction becomes a gaze, we are headed for trouble. We cannot keep our spirit encouraged by looking in the wrong direction.

In order to maintain our vision, we also must maintain our joy. When David was discouraged, he put his hope in God. How exactly did he do this? He was basically an outlaw on the run, isolated from humanity. His enemies were pursuing him on every side. He couldn't turn on TBN to listen to an edifying sermon. He couldn't call someone for prayer. He couldn't even open his Bible for a word from the Lord. Everything he did to encourage himself was initiated by disciplining his thoughts. A thought that brought fear or discouragement or self-pity was replaced. He chose the thoughts he allowed entrance. He began with purposeful reflection of God's character. He restricted his mind to meditate only on thoughts that would uplift him. He reminded himself of former victories. He recalled good times with the Lord. Slowly, the discouragement faded and hope filled the vacancy.

When we train our minds to reject negative thoughts, we position ourselves for victory. This principle of restricting the unqualified is utilized in many areas of life. Mortgage companies reject loan applicants with low credit scores due to the increased risk of default. They have a bottom line to protect. Foreclosures will reduce the strength and profitability of the company. Employers reject applicants who don't have the necessary background and job skills. Unqualified employees will slow down business operations and cause exponential problems. And even though the next example is a worldly illustration, it provides the best visual aid for the point I'm trying to make. Exclusive Hollywood clubs only admit members of certain ranks. They even have a muscle-bound bouncer at the door to enforce their policy. Why is this so strictly enforced? The club's strength and profitability is directly related to the ranks of those allowed entrance.

The strength and profitability of your mind is directly tied to the ranks of the thoughts you allow access. Wouldn't it be great if you had a muscle-bound bouncer at the entrance of your mind to kick out unacceptable thoughts? You do! The Holy Spirit. He is your advisor. He will tell you if a thought is unacceptable. He will even tell you if the thought was merely disguised as a good thought. But then it is up to you to replace your thoughts so that your mind will be occupied with goodness. Your mind is your most valuable asset. Do everything possible to equip it and strengthen yourself from the enemy's attacks.

Recognizing the Bait

A fisherman knows that a fish will not bite an ordinary hook, so he baits the hook with something attractive to the fish he wants to catch. He completely conceals the hook with something alluring to the fish so that all the fish will see is the lure. Satan baits us the same way. A partial truth covers and conceals a lie. He uses truth like bait to hide the hook—the lie.

Not all fish like the same bait so the fisherman has to select the particular kind of bait for the particular kind of fish. Likewise, Satan studies us. He knows our weaknesses and places of vulnerability. He knows exactly what to entice you with and when to catch you off guard. He won't attack you when you are strong. He waits for an opportune time. He did the same thing with Jesus. Satan waited until Jesus was hungry, lonely, and tired in the desert before he approached Him. And he will wait until you are weak, lonely, and hungry before he baits you.

He also knows that not all of us will be enticed by the same lure.

If you are having marital issues, Satan may tempt you with thoughts of leaving. He may even use live bait—Mr. Tall, Dark, and Handsome. Or he may use Mr. Short, Blonde, and Rich. Whatever turns you on. If you are single but dissatisfied with your relationship status, Satan may convince you that any relationship is better than none at all. Be on guard. Make sure you have some girlfriends who know how to listen and pray on speed dial. Even Jesus needed ministry. After He was tempted by the devil in the wilderness, angels came and attended to Him (Matthew 4:11).

You Are What You Think

Creating fantasies or vain imaginations is dangerous. Why? Because the Bible says that as a woman thinks in her heart, so shall she be (Proverbs 23:7). Our thoughts create what we become. You've probably heard the expression, "You are what you eat." In a similar way, this Scripture tells us we are what we think.

We become what we think because feelings grow from our thoughts. And feelings eventually manifest actions. It all starts with a thought. If you want godly actions, you must plant godly thoughts. If you want to change your actions, change your thoughts. If you want to change your emotions, change your thoughts. Thoughts are the seed.

If you are tempted to obsess over romance in your thought life, it's time to take your thoughts captive and plant some new ones. "Finally, brothers, whatever is true, whatever is noble, whatever is right, whatever is pure, whatever is lovely, whatever is admirable— if anything is excellent or praiseworthy—think about such things" (Philippians 4:8).

If you feed your spirit thoughts that are based on the standards set forth in Philippians 4:8, then you will be spiritually healthy. If, however, you meditate on things that are not worthy of praise and do not agree with God's Word, then you must submit them to the obedience of Christ.

We aren't responsible for the tempting thoughts that present themselves to us, but we are responsible for the thoughts we welcome and entertain. We don't have to yield to the temptation. We can discern the difference between a good thought and a bad thought by measuring it against the Word. If the thought contradicts the Word, reject it. If the thought provokes feelings that do not honor God, discard it. If the thought causes you to create a mind movie that takes you into fantasy, submit that thought to the obedience of Christ and discipline your mind to think on things above.

Remember that you cannot remove thoughts from your mind, and it is impossible to just stop thinking. Have you ever tried to think about nothing? It's impossible. Something is always going through your mind. When thoughts that don't honor God present themselves to you, don't think that you can simply erase them. You have to replace them. First, you must surrender them to the obedience of Christ, and then replace them with something that honors God.

Be Careful What You Feed

There is a story about an old Cherokee who was telling his grandson about a battle that goes on inside people's minds. He explained the conflict to his grandson this way...

> *"My son, the battle is between the two 'wolves' inside us all. One is Evil. It is anger, envy, jealousy, sorrow, regret, greed, arrogance, self-pity, guilt, resentment, inferiority, lies, false pride, superiority, and ego. The other is Good. It is joy, peace,*

love, hope, serenity, humility, kindness, benevolence, empathy, generosity, truth, compassion, and faith."

The grandson thought about it for a minute and then asked his grandfather, "Which wolf wins?"

The old Cherokee replied, "The one you feed."

Replacing our thoughts takes discipline and is difficult at first. Fantasizing is a habit, but it can be broken. You break it the same way you embraced it—by fixing your mind on a thought, only in reverse. What you feed grows. What you starve dies. Thoughts are the same way. The more you think about something the more intensely you feel the feelings associated with those thoughts.

Determine in advance what thoughts you will meditate on when you are tempted to fantasize. Having an arsenal of pure thoughts will help you when tempting thoughts cause paralysis of analysis. In the heat of the battle of your mind, you won't have much time to think about how to redirect your thoughts. It's a lot easier to redirect your thoughts when you already have replacements ready. When the tempting thought presents itself, discipline your mind to think about the righteous thought until the other one goes away.

Martin Luther said, "You can't keep a bird from flying over your head, but you can prevent him from building a nest." Redirecting disappointment and unhealthy thoughts is vital to breaking the toxic love cycle. A healthy thought life is essential in order to follow God's vision for your future.

-13-

Mind Affairs

"EACH ONE IS TEMPTED WHEN, BY HIS OWN EVIL
DESIRE, HE IS DRAGGED AWAY AND ENTICED."
JAMES 1:14

HAVE YOU EVER HAD A MIND AFFAIR? A romance novel featuring you and Mr. Handsome Hunk? A chick flick starring you with Robert Pattinson or Brad Pitt? Or maybe yours is an imaginary rendezvous with someone only famous in your own little world.

There is a fine line between friendship and emotional affairs. So how do you tell if you are having a mind affair? Jeanne Mayo, president of Youth Leader's Coach, says an emotional affair is having emotional needs met by a person that only Christ or your spouse should meet. Check the list below. If any of the following occur, you might be having an emotional affair.

1. You anticipate spending time with him (even if it's online or at church)

2. You go out of your way to run into him

3. You find ways to impress him

4. Sexual tension exists

5. You fantasize about him

6. You compare him to other men

7. If you're married, you compare him to your spouse

8. You think about him more than your spouse

9. You feel he understands you—"gets" you—better than your spouse

10. As we began listing these items, you began to justify your actions. Well, that's me, but ...

IS A MIND AFFAIR REALLY DANGEROUS?

In my ministry work with singles, I've heard numerous stories from women who are having an emotional affair. Some women fantasize about a man who doesn't even know their name, while others imagine a life of romantic bliss with a coworker they barely know. Women with relationship addiction tendencies take mind affairs to an obsessive level. Their imagination is consumed with thoughts and dreams not surrendered to the Lord. They mentally plan their wedding, where they will live, and how many children they will have.

Women caught up in mind affairs have trouble distinguishing between fantasy and reality, and often are convinced they have heard from God. Their discernment is distorted by their own obsession. They have made a love interest an idol of the heart. Married women can have emotional affairs as well. They are especially vulnerable when seasons of their marriage become ordinary and mundane.

Women with relationship addiction tendencies take mind affairs to an obsessive level.

Maybe the thrill is gone. Maybe unresolved issues in your marriage are straining your last nerve. Maybe you are struggling with the responsibility of changing diapers and putting your career on hold, or maybe your babies have left for college and you suddenly find yourself devoid of affection and purpose. Maybe you are hungry, tired, and lonely.

Lysa TerKeurst, president of Proverbs 31 Ministries, tells about a married woman who was caught off guard by an emotional affair:

> "A few years ago, I watched a friend get tangled up in an emotional affair. She was a strong Christian woman who loved her family, but the attraction to this other man seemed unavoidable. She tried to talk herself out of it, but her heart played tricks on her mind, and the justifications for letting things continue down this path soon led her to a very dangerous place. She was becoming emotionally attached to this other man."

Out of desperation and fear, the woman confided in Lysa what was going on. "As she described how she got pulled into this place, I found myself being challenged by the realization of how subtly this had happened. She hadn't planned on being emotionally attracted to this other man. As a matter of fact, she'd always prided herself on being a woman of strong conviction and had scoffed at the idea of ever being tempted to have an affair."

Lysa recognized from this woman's story how subtly such relationships begin and evolve.

> *"It starts off simple enough—his comment that you mull over one too many times, a conversation in which you find a surprising connection, a glance that lingers just a second too long, or one of a thousand other interactions that seem innocent yet aren't. These are the dangerous seeds that can easily sprout into an emotional affair."*[18]

An emotional affair not surrendered to the Lord can easily turn into a physical affair, but even if it doesn't get that far, an emotional affair will divide your affections and cause disappointment with your current situation or relationship.

IS A MIND AFFAIR ADULTERY?

Diane had never considered engaging in an adulterous relationship, yet she had many mind affairs. Daydreaming about Dennis, the handsome chief financial officer at work, she wondered what it would be like to be his wife.

"I saw the pictures he had neatly displayed in his office—his botoxed wife and private-schooled children were proudly displayed on his bookshelf like trophies. Every day, I saw him walk in the front door. It was always the same time—8:45. I made it a point to be at my desk. I didn't want to miss his greeting. 'Good morning, Diane,' he would say with a casual smile and wink. He was only being friendly, but to me, that little wink meant so much more."

Soon Diane found herself replacing his wife's face with her face on his wall of fame. Diane soon discovered that emotional adultery and emotional affairs can be just as destructive as a physical affair. Thoughts of Dennis consumed her. At first, her symptoms were mild disappointment. She thought she'd never find someone as perfect as Dennis. She was right. The next three men she dated didn't stand a chance. None of them could measure up to the fantasy she'd created in her head.

Just because Diane never indulged in a physical affair doesn't mean she wasn't guilty of adultery. Under the New Covenant, it's possible to be innocent of physical adultery but be guilty of entertaining adulterous thoughts. Jesus makes it clear in Matthew 5:28 that the act of adultery begins in the mind: "But I tell you that anyone who looks at a woman [or man] lustfully has already committed adultery with her [or him] in his heart."

To lust means to desire something eagerly, to long for something or someone, or to have an unlawful desire of carnal pleasure. It's not just about a sexual appetite, and men aren't the only ones who lust. For women struggling with relationship addiction, emotional affairs are common and even more dangerous to their emotional health. I challenge you to consider a paraphrase of Matthew 5:28:

"But I tell you that any woman who fantasizes, longs for, or yearns for a man, relationship, or romance lustfully has already committed adultery with him in her heart."

You may think this is a harsh statement— and it is—but the reason emotional adultery is so dangerous is because an emotional affair will grow out of control if the fire is not put out. The more we think about something, feelings begin to surface. The more we

> *The more we think about something, feelings begin to surface. The more we feel, the more we want.*

feel, the more we want. The more we want, the more our resolve diminishes. And then what began as a thought has grown into full action. The bottom line is that an act of physical adultery always begins in the mind.

Jesus said in Matthew 15:19, "For out of the heart proceed evil thoughts, murders, adulteries, fornications, thefts, false witness, blasphemies." He knew the progressive nature of sin. That's why he considered an unyielded lustful thought in the same category as adultery.

As soon as you recognize that a thought contradicts the promises or commands in the Bible, pluck that arrow out! Take that thought captive like a prisoner and surrender it to the only one who can handle the enemy—Christ.

THE POWER OF CONFESSION

I've found one of the greatest ways to combat the temptation to ponder the affections of another man is to confess it to a trusted friend who won't be judgmental. In my case, I confess mine to my husband. I am fully committed to John and I know beyond a shadow of a doubt that God brought us together, but I never want to give the enemy an ounce of opportunity to set me up. I know how much I struggled in the past with my relationship addiction that made me crave the affection and approval of other men. Even though we've been married for over fifteen years, as much as I'd like to think I've matured past the point of further temptation, I realize there will never be a time when I can let go of my boundaries.

The apostle Paul warned in 1 Corinthians 10:12, "So, if you think you are standing firm, be careful that you don't fall!" Here's the truth of the matter: The moment I think I've arrived is the moment I'm most vulnerable. It's because my spirit is willing but the flesh is weak. Jesus urged us to "watch and pray so that you will not fall into temptation" (Matthew 26:41).

Just because you're married or in a committed relationship doesn't mean there will never be another man you find attractive. Like Tom, a friend of my husband once said, "The first look is free. The second one costs."

That's why I told my husband about Brad (not his real name). Brad was the husband of a friend of mine, and the four of us occasionally went out to eat together. Brad was charismatic, handsome and tall, exactly the type of man I most often fell for in the past. One day I ran into him at church and sensed that he crossed the line with his charm. He was flirting with me. But here's the honest truth. I liked it.

Of course sin feels good. Those who say it doesn't are lying. That's the way Satan baits us. None of us would ever take the bait if sin didn't feel good. I knew I had to tell John. For one thing, I wanted him to guard me whenever Brad was around again. I wanted John to stake his claim, and I trusted that I could tell John my honest thoughts. Actually, telling John about Brad strengthened our trust even more. To disclose something this vulnerable increased our intimacy. But the most dramatic thing that happened when I told John was something I never expected.

As soon as I told John about my weakness, it literally evaporated. I never again thought Brad attractive. His looks didn't change. His charm stayed the same and he didn't shrink in stature, but the exposure of my weakness to the light strengthened me. This is one time I experienced what the apostle Paul meant when He said, "My grace is sufficient for you, for my power is made perfect in weakness . . . when I am weak, then I am strong" (2 Corinthians 12:9).

> *Full disclosure is a powerful antidote for unhealthy thoughts. Once darkness is exposed to the light, it loses its power over us.*

Whether you are married or single, if you struggle with mind affairs, I urge you to confess them to a trusted friend or counselor or to God in repentant prayer. Full disclosure is a powerful antidote for unhealthy thoughts. Once darkness is exposed to the light, it loses its power over us. Proverbs 28:13 says, "Whoever conceals their sins does not prosper, but the one who confesses and renounces them finds mercy." If you are married and your relationship with your husband is strong enough to handle this type of disclosure, find a quiet time to discuss it with him. Due to the nature of the confession, however, I would recommend you first pray about how and when God wants you to discuss it with your partner. Always remember: When secrets live, intimacy dies, but when intimacy lives, secrets die.

—14—

Strengthening Your Imagination

CONTROLLING YOUR IMAGINATION can feel like a battle in your brain. That's because it is. Satan's arrows are evil imaginations aimed at your brain, only they don't always seem evil. That's because he camouflages the tip of the arrow with an attractive, seemingly innocent thought. If he can penetrate your mind with that thought, he can pollute your imagination.

The book of Ephesians compares this battle in our imagination to the armor worn in battle by Roman soldiers (see chapter six). Interestingly, none of the Roman armor mentioned in Ephesians covered the back side. As long as soldiers faced their enemy, they were protected, but if they turned and ran away, the enemy was sure to gain advantage. In the same way, you can use your armor, the word of truth, to face your enemy and defeat his lies. The following Scriptures, action points, and questions to ponder will help you strengthen your imagination so you can maintain a healthy thought life and follow God's vision for your future.

IMAGINATION SCRIPTURE TRUTHS

✦ "As a man thinketh in his heart, so is he" (Proverbs 23:7 KJV).

✦ "Do not conform any longer to the pattern of this world, but be transformed by the renewing of your mind. Then you will be able to test and approve what God's will is—his good, pleasing and perfect will" (Romans 12:2).

✦ "Casting down imaginations, and every high thing that exalteth itself against the knowledge of God, and bringing into captivity every thought to the obedience of Christ" (2 Corinthians 10:5 KJV).

✦ "Finally, brothers, whatever is true, whatever is noble, whatever is right, whatever is pure, whatever is lovely, whatever is admirable—if anything is excellent or praiseworthy—think about such things" (Philippians 4:8).

✦ "Where there is no revelation, people cast off restraint" (Proverbs 29:18).

✦ "What I feared has come upon me; what I dreaded has happened to me" (Job 3:25).

✦ "There is no wisdom, no insight, no plan that can succeed against the LORD" (Proverbs 21:30).

✦ "Be strong and very courageous. Be careful to obey all the law my servant Moses gave you; do not turn from it to the right or to the left, that you may be successful wherever you go" (Joshua 1:7).

✦ "Surely the Sovereign Lord does nothing without revealing his plan to his servants the prophets" (Amos 3:7).

IMAGINATION ACTION POINTS

To strengthen your imagination, try the following action points to replace vain imaginations with truth.

Pray for God's Vision

If you were going on a trip, you wouldn't head out on the road unless you knew where you were going. You would use MapQuest or your GPS to plot your course. Why not ask for guidance on this journey of life? It's the biggest trip you'll ever take, and yet so many of us wander around not knowing exactly where we are going, hoping we'll arrive somewhere nice. We may eventually get where we're supposed to be, but it takes three times as long to get there.

Ask God to open your eyes and give you His vision for your future. Amos 3:7 says, "Surely the Sovereign Lord does nothing without revealing his plan to his servants the prophets." In the Old Testament, God spoke through His prophets, but in the New Testament, the Holy Spirit speaks to all of us. Therefore, today we have the capacity to pray and ask for divine direction. When we have God's vision for our future, it's so much easier to proceed with confidence.

In my first marriage, many people wondered why, after I confessed my sin of adultery and allowed God to restore my life, I continued to tolerate my husband's drug and pornography addiction and verbal abuse for another eight years. Although it was difficult, I believed the decision wasn't up to me. I had clear vision from God that He was restoring my life. God confirmed this to me through personal Scriptures, dreams, and an inner knowing. If I intentionally went against the awareness of His will, I would have forfeited the grace God gave me to endure. As I stayed under the shelter of the Most High, He empowered me to walk in love despite my circumstances. If I had chosen to abort God's plan, my situation may have improved, but my peace would have evaporated and I would have missed something vital God was trying to accomplish in my life. For one thing, God was not done with *me* yet. He was perfecting me through the adversity I endured.

When we don't allow perseverance to finish its work (James 1:4), the unresolved issues in our lives often produce bitterness, sorrow, despair, and depression. These are not the fruits God intends to work into our lives. These are the fruits that develop when we give up before the promise manifests. Giving up prematurely is like taking a cake out of the oven after only ten minutes—we're left with a sticky, gooey mess. But when we endure to the end, we get to experience the promise on the other side of our pain.

Scripture tells us, "And the God of all grace, who called you to his eternal glory in Christ, after you have suffered a little while, will himself restore you and make you strong, firm and steadfast" (1 Peter 5:10). There is a promise on the other side of your suffering. God is in the middle of some refining work. You are His work in progress. Through your issues, He is restoring, confirming, strengthening, and establishing you.

The apostle Paul writes in Romans 5:3, "Not only so, but we also glory in our sufferings, because we know that suffering produces perseverance; perseverance, character; and character, hope." Other versions of Romans 5:3 use different words to describe the outcome of our sufferings, words like patience, endurance and steadfastness. The *New Living Translation* puts it this way: "We can rejoice, too, when we run into problems and trials, for we know that they are good for us—they help us learn to endure."

Here's the bottom line: Hope is the end result of suffering. In other words, in order to receive hope we have to pass through perseverance and character. Trying to get hope without developing our endurance and experience would be like an Olympian expecting to win a gold metal without training and refining her skills.

Hope is the fruit that is produced *after* our character and endurance is developed. Hope is the prize we receive when we suffer and prevail. Today, because of adversity in my life, and because I surrendered to the work of God and allowed Him to develop my perseverance and character, I have tremendous hope.

While I was married to Tom, I never took my eyes off the vision that God was restoring my life. At the time, I truly believed God was restoring my marriage as well. To focus my thoughts on anything else would not have produced good fruit in my life. But one day after ten years of marriage, I felt a release. It wasn't something I prayed for. It wasn't brought on by my own request. Rather, it was a distinct feeling in my spirit that God acknowledged I had done all I could and He was releasing me from my marriage. Today, I am grateful for the conflict I endured. I am not the same woman I once was. I am filled with hope and am no longer bitter. I know without a shadow of a doubt, if I had left my marriage before God released me, He would not have been able to grow that fruit in me.

What about you? While I do believe that far too many women abandon a marriage or committed relationship before God's work is finished, clearly not every adverse situation is something God intends for you to endure. That's why it's so important that you get God's clear direction for your own situation. Pray for God's vision. I believe He'll not only answer, but equip you with the peace you need to endure the journey He has planned for you.

Judge the Fruit of Your Thoughts

Some thoughts seem harmless at the time, so it's hard to discern whether or not they're a healthy meditation. One of the best ways to examine your thoughts is to think about what they will produce in the future. Our thoughts eventually turn into beliefs, so consider what your thoughts will produce when they grow up and mature. What will their belief look like? Will they produce the fruits of the spirit like joy, peace, or patience, or will they manifest as anxiety, discontent, jealousy, or hatred (Galatians 5:19-22)?

Our thoughts should line up with Scripture. When we internalize destructive thoughts, often the very thing we fear happens. Job acknowledged this in his own suffering when he said, "What I feared has come upon me; what I dreaded has happened to me" (3:25). Psychologists call this concept the Pygmalion effect or a self-fulfilling prophecy in which our internalized expectations actually come to pass. That's even more reason to discipline ourselves to think on things that will produce life. If you have a hard time examining your thoughts on your own, discuss them with a mature Christian friend who can help you judge the fruit of your thoughts.

Pinpoint False Beliefs

In the action points on identity, we evaluated our thoughts to eliminate negative thoughts we had about ourselves. It's also important to renew your mind about false beliefs you may have about your circumstances. Just like a house gathers dust, your mind can be full of hidden beliefs that clutter its recesses. In Mark chapter eleven, Jesus saw a fig tree without any fruit and commanded the fig tree to wither and die. Often Jesus used physical acts to demonstrate spiritual principles. Commanding a fig tree to wither and die is symbolic of removing the things in our life that aren't producing fruit. Likewise, we are to take authority over beliefs that aren't producing life.

When Allysa heard me teach on this subject, she raised her hand to comment. "I understand the importance of getting rid of false beliefs, but my mind wanders too much. I'll never be able to take every thought captive." Allysa startled herself. As soon as she made her confession, she realized she had pinpointed a false belief. "I can't believe that's what I've been thinking," she said. "Saying it out loud made it easier to see the falsehood. I'm replacing that thought because the truth is I have the mind of Christ."

Try saying your thoughts out loud to help you identify hidden beliefs. You may be surprised. Until you hear them spoken, you may not realize how many false beliefs occupy your mind. Lurking in the quiet recesses of your brain, they can be silent killers. Expose and destroy toxic beliefs, then replace them with God's truth.

Write Replacement Thoughts

Do you remember writing out sentences in grade school? Writing them out helps reinforce the thoughts in your brain. It takes a lot of repetition to change habitual thoughts.

When your thoughts don't line up with Scripture, deliberately consider alternative thoughts. Plan ahead of time what truths you will meditate on, so that whenever you find yourself tempted with negative thoughts, you can immediately focus on the truth. Like practicing a fire drill, you don't wait until a fire comes to figure out your plan of escape. You practice it beforehand so you will know what to do in a time of emergency.

As Dr. Caroline Leaf says, "The actual process of writing consolidates the memory and adds clarity to what you have been thinking about. It helps you see more clearly the areas that need detoxing, because it literally allows you to look at your brain on paper. Writing helps you see your non-conscious and conscious thoughts in a visual way."[19]

Declare the Truth to Yourself

This exercise is awkward at first because we're often told that only crazy people talk to themselves. I dare you to do it anyway! Try this when you're alone. Look in the mirror and speak truth to yourself. Something happens when you look into your own eyes and speak life-giving words. The truth is energizing. It's like an instant charge of power entering the windows of your own soul. Speaking the truth empowers you to believe it about yourself. Remember, you cannot achieve victory unless you can first imagine it, but when you perceive it you can receive it.

Live in the Moment

It's so important to live each moment of today and yet far too many of us live in the future, dreading what might happen. Anxiety about financial problems in my first marriage consumed me. I stayed so focused on what might happen tomorrow that any peace for the present completely vanished. I obsessed my thoughts on tomorrow. *Would the electricity be cut off? How would I buy groceries?*

A friend suggested that I begin by replacing my fear and anxiety with God's truth. Let me explain the difference between *fact* and *truth*. Facts are based on what we see with our eyes. Facts are rooted in our circumstances. We become discouraged when we deceive ourselves by believing our circumstances. The fact was that our bank account was low, but God's truth trumps facts. God's truth says that He shall supply all of our needs (Philippians 4:19). As I focused on truth, I realized how futile it was to worry about tomorrow when today I had everything I needed.

The truth was that *today* I had electricity. *Today* my family had food to eat. I aligned my thoughts according to 2 Peter 1:3, "Today I have everything I need for life and godliness." I meditated on the fact that today all my needs were supplied. And guess what happened? I gradually started believing what I declared and my peace increased. I was able to enjoy time with my family because my focus was on the provision of today and not what my fears projected.

Worrying about tomorrow invokes fear and destroys our peace today (Matthew 6:34). When you live in the moment and align your imagination with God's truth, you will experience a stronger sense of peace.

Give Discouragement a Time Limit

Have you ever noticed that the only one who wants to come to your pity party is you? If you frequently find yourself down and out, one of the worst things you can tell yourself is to "just get over it." Instead, give yourself a time limit to pout and then be done with it. You might even try setting the buzzer for ten minutes, then sit down and allow yourself to sulk. Pour out your complaints to God, but when the buzzer goes off, leave the pity party as you silence it. Then offer up a sacrifice of praise—intentionally give God praise whether you feel like it or not. Just like it's difficult to smile and be mad, it's also hard to give praise and sulk at the same time because feelings follow actions.

After you've released your cares to God, if you find that you've taken back the burden once again, simply repeat the process. God will never grow weary of listening to your prayers, and He loves hearing your praises. If you continue this practice, over time you should notice that your discouragement has decreased.

Practice Breath Prayers

Breathing exercises are a way to promote deep relaxation and reduce anxiety. Combining this physical act of breathing with the spiritual practice of prayer is known by some as "breath prayer." Start by finding a quiet place where you can be still before God. Slow down your breathing by taking a few deep breaths. Inhale deeply, hold it a moment and slowly exhale. The book of Genesis says that God breathed the breath of life into Adam and he became a living being, so as you inhale, consider that you are breathing in God's presence. As you exhale, consider that you are ridding your body of toxic thoughts, releasing your anxiety and cares to the Lord, and relinquishing control over your concerns.

Add to your breathing exercise a short passage of Scripture. For example, as you meditate on Joshua 1:7, breathe in and think or tell yourself, *I am strong.* As you exhale, say aloud or whisper, "I am courageous." Inhale again while you meditate, *I am careful to obey* . . . exhale as you say, "all the law." Inhale again as you tell yourself, *I am successful* . . . exhale as you state, "wherever I go." Breath prayers are a powerful way to engage your body with your mind in meditation at the same time.

Memorize Scriptures

Find and memorize Scriptures that counteract the lies you struggle with. Write them down, think about them, speak them out loud, or say them to yourself in the mirror. Write a few of your favorites on note cards and put them in your purse or car. You can also post them on your mirror or refrigerator—anywhere you will see them frequently. "The Word of God is living and active and sharper than a two-edged sword" (Hebrews 4:12).

QUESTIONS TO PONDER

+ How do you tell the difference between vain imaginations and truth?

+ If you are single, what are the signs that you are having a mind affair? What if you are married? Are the standards different?

+ Based on what you've read, what is the difference between fantasy and imagination?

✦ What role do your thoughts play in predicting your actions?

✦ When you want to change your behavior, why is it important to visualize the change?

✦ What person or people in the Bible utilized the habit of imagination? Did it help or hinder their situation?

✦ Can we control our thoughts? How much?

✦ How does Satan bait us to embrace a lie? Are his temptations complete lies?

✦ What advice would you give a single girlfriend who is meeting men online?

The writer of Ephesians doesn't tell a soldier to go and fight after he is dressed for battle. Instead he is told several times to stand firm. When you take your position, face your enemy, and refuse his lies—the Lord fights your battle for you. Your responsibility is to stand. There is, however, one final instruction to win the battle in your imagination: Pray on all occasions. And that brings us to the next step to breaking the toxic love cycle: Embracing the habit of prayer. Are you ready to get fully dressed for battle?

-15-

STEP NUMBER 4:
Prayer

PRAYER: THE PRACTICE OF CONVERSING WITH GOD
TO SEEK DIRECTION AND WISDOM.

DO YOU HAVE SCRIPTURES you don't like? I do, and
they are both from Psalms: "Wait for the Lord" (27:14) and "Be
still and know that I am God" (46:10).

These verses have guilt-inducing properties for two reasons.
First, I'm a borderline hyper-maniac, so it goes against my nature
to wait and be still. But I think the main reason I never bonded
with these verses is because I had several misconceptions about
what it means to wait and be still. I used to think prayer was a silent activity—a moment of quiet reflection. I conjured up images
of humming monks or prostrate priests and measured my prayer
performance against my perception of their spiritual standards.
The truth is, often my mind wandered during prayer, or worse,
I fell asleep. How could I be an effective Christian and flunk
prayer?

PART OF WAITING IS SERVING

For years, I misunderstood what waiting really meant. I thought waiting was a long pause or a period of passive inactivity, like being put on hold. But waiting isn't passive—waiting is full of action. If you don't believe me, get a job waiting tables. You'll never have a moment to rest. Waitresses and waiters are some of the busiest people I know. They take orders, serve meals, clean up messes, and constantly watch to see if their customers need anything else. Likewise, while we are waiting on the Lord, we should be active. What if we approached our prayer time as a time to ask God what He wanted? What if we served Him, cleaned up messes, and checked back to see what else He needed?

When the Bible says to "wait on the Lord" it actually means to minister before Him. In fact, check this out: The word *minister* comes from the Greek word *diakonos,* which means a servant or a waiter, one who executes the commands of another. Waiting is our active part in serving Him.

As we wait on the Lord and minister before Him, He does something extraordinary. According to Psalm 27:14, in the midst of our waiting, He strengthens us. "Wait on the Lord: be of good courage, and he shall strengthen thine heart: wait, I say, on the Lord" (KJV). If you are waiting on Him to heal your marriage or bring your mate, don't get weary. Even if it seems like nothing is happening, He is faithful.

PART OF WAITING IS EXPECTING

To this day I don't sit still or play the waiting game very well, but it was a great awakening when I recognized another truth about prayer. Part of waiting is expecting. If you've ever been pregnant, this aspect of waiting will be easy to understand because it's a busy time when you're expecting a baby. You'll probably make several trips to the doctor, purchase clothing and baby furniture, decorate the baby's room, and most importantly, pick out a name. You don't just sit around and wait for labor pains because you *expect* the baby to come. If all you're doing is chilling and hanging out you won't be prepared when the baby comes.

Esther was a woman of prayer, and she understood both how to wait for the Lord and how to be still. The book of Esther describes her dilemma. Under the evil advice of Haman, one of the king's nobles, the king had signed a law to destroy all the Jews, but he didn't know Queen Esther, his new wife, was a Jew. Esther *had* to speak to the king. Her life and the lives of her people depended on it. Yet, without being summoned by the king, it was forbidden to approach him. Unless he lowered his scepter, the punishment was death.

Esther prayed and called her people to pray. Thankfully, when she approached his throne, the king lowered his scepter. He even offered to give her up to half of his kingdom, but because Esther had covered the situation in prayer, she wasn't hasty. Even though the "labor pains" of her dilemma were intense, something in her spirit knew it wasn't yet time. A request at this point would have been premature. Instead, she waited. Then she offered to prepare the king a banquet. Again, after the banquet, the king offered Esther half of his kingdom; but like a doctor who sees a baby crowning and tells the mother to wait, she knew it still wasn't quite yet time to deliver her request.

The next evening Haman's evil plot was discovered without Esther's need to make an accusation. I believe it was because Esther knew prayer involved being still and waiting. If she had allowed impatience to cause her to make her request prematurely, the story would probably have had a different ending. Instead, God's will prevailed and the Jews were saved from destruction.

We can learn a lot about prayer from Esther's story. Esther didn't pray and rush ahead of God. She waited on His timing. What if we arrive at the place or season or relationship we've been waiting for, but we miss the opportunity because we didn't prepare while we were waiting? Or what if we arrive at the relationship God wants for us, but we rush the process and proceed ahead of God's timing? No doubt, there will be issues in the relationship we are unprepared for. Like a premature baby incubated in the hospital, we may have to nurse the relationship until it can thrive on its own. Esther also understood her marriage and God-given position as queen was not just for her own comfort. God had elevated her for kingdom purposes. Likewise, God has a kingdom purpose, not only for you, but for your marriage as well. Don't give up on your dream to be a confident, soul-healthy woman. Allow God to use the hard places of your life to prepare you for what He wants to do with you and your husband or your future husband as a team.

PRAYER IS NOT SILENT

One day, while sitting at my kitchen table having my quiet time, the thought crossed my mind, *You should march around your house while you pray.*

Excuse me? I scoffed at my own idea. *How ridiculous is that?*

Ignoring the notion, I continued my prayer. "Dear Lord, please bless ..."

But then the thought came again. *You should march around your house while you pray.*

I had heard this voice before. It sounded just like me. Surely, it was a crazy Christy thought, so once again I discounted the idea and went back to my prayers. But the annoying interruption persisted.

By now, I was super irritated. What was this silly voice in my head talking about? A Jericho march? I was certain it was nothing more than a distraction to my quiet time.

But ...

What if it wasn't?

What if the still small voice was God?

Nah!

As ridiculous as it sounded, however, I realized there was only one way to silence it. *OK. Fine,* I thought. *I'll do it—just to get rid of this silly notion. If that will shut up my mind then maybe I can get on with my* quiet *time.*

At least no one was home.

I stood up and lifted my right foot. Memories of teaching my children Christian kids' songs with motions sprung to my mind. *I may never march in the infantry, ride in the cavalry, shoot the artillery ...*

I'm not a three-year-old! I insisted to no one but myself.

I lifted my left foot.

I'm a grown adult!

The march was on.

I checked the windows in my living room. I hoped my neighbors couldn't see. Surely they would wonder why this crazy Christian woman was marching around her house and talking to herself.

I scuffled around the circular path that connected my kitchen and living room. "Dear Lord, I thank you for your provision and this beautiful day." *At least the silly voice is leaving me alone now.* "Thank you that You hear my prayers—that You know the plans You have for my family."

After the second trip around my house, concern that someone might see me left. After the third trip, I began to feel more energy and passion in my prayers. My concentration was more focused. For one thing, there was no way I could drift off to sleep while marching and walking, which I often did when I prayed sitting down with my eyes closed. After the fourth trip around, I felt a powerful connection. My prayers were in motion. They were active. They were alive and powerful. They were sharper than a two-edged sword. I felt engaged and energized.

I learned a powerful lesson that day. An activity that I had discounted as being ridiculous was revolutionary to my prayer life. I felt the power Joshua must have felt as he marched around Jericho. With each step he took, the spirit of God infused him with vision.

Maybe you're like me. All too often, I've reduced prayer to a silent routine and settled for a mundane monotony, thinking the only effective prayer is the kind where we bow our heads and close our eyes. Absolutely, there is a time for reverence, but there are so many other ways to pray. We can't put God in a box and think that's the only way we can connect with Him and hear His voice. He is far more creative than that.

Consider trying a Jericho march. Or simply take a walk outside and talk to God. When the beauty of His nature surrounds you it shoves out the distractions of life. I know many people have great conversations with God outdoors while experiencing His beauty. It's amazing how the extraction of electronics can help us hear His voice better.

Maybe you hear God's voice most clearly when you sing or listen to music. Crank up the stereo and talk to God. Whatever helps you communicate with God—do that. Prayer is a dialogue with your creator. It's a two-way conversation, an exchange of thoughts between a loving God and His child—and an essential part of becoming a soul-healthy woman.

-16-

Trust Your Gut

"TRUSTING OUR INTUITION OFTEN
SAVES US FROM DISASTER."
—ANNE WILSON SCHAEF

OFTEN WOMEN WHO SETTLE FOR unhealthy relationships have learned to ignore their inner witness. When a gut feeling tells them a guy isn't right for them, they ignore or minimize it. When a woman ignores her instinct, or the witness of the Holy Spirit guiding her with discernment, she is headed for trouble.

Learn to trust your gut. God longs to speak to you. With that in mind, let's talk about six things we can do to position ourselves so that we're more likely to hear His voice and trust our inner witness.

DON'T MONOPOLIZE THE CONVERSATION

As a young Christian, I was a nonstop chatterbox. My prayer life consisted of blurting out my requests to God and shouting,

"Amen!" That would have been like calling my best friend on the phone and spilling out everything I wanted to say and then announcing, "Hey, it was great talking to you ... gotta go, see you later, *bye!*"

Click.

Of course, I never did that with my friends, but I did it all the time with God. My friends would be shocked if they didn't get a chance to speak. I think that's how God felt. He had so many things He wanted to tell me, but I never stayed on the line long enough to listen.

I thought prayer was only about my petitions and pleas and talking to God was my chance to make requests. Making requests, however, is only one aspect of prayer. In his book *Experiencing God,* Henry Blackaby writes, "Prayer is two-way fellowship and communication with God. You speak to God and He speaks to you."[20] Prayer actually means communication with God, and communication is never just one way. Don't make the same mistake I once did and reduce prayer to a monologue. Prayer is a two-way conversation, and God longs to talk to you.

LEARN TO LISTEN

Listening is not the same as hearing. Let me explain. I used to keep my television on all day just to keep me company. Most of the time I never sat still long enough to hear one word that came across the channel. I could even be in the same room as the television and still not listen to it because I tuned it out. Just because I wasn't listening, however, didn't mean the program wasn't continuing to air.

I used to give God about as much attention as I did my television. God could be talking to me all day long, but I never heard a word He spoke to me. When I finally started listening to God's voice, I realized that He had been talking to me for years, but I had ignored Him. I didn't hear His voice because I never sat still long enough to listen.

I didn't have a hearing problem—I had a listening problem.

Our failure to listen doesn't stop God from speaking to us anymore than it stops our television, cable networks, and internet from broadcasting. We make the choice whether or not to listen or hit the mute button. One of my favorite Scriptures is John 10:27: "My sheep hear my voice and I know them and they follow me." Notice, it doesn't say we *might* hear His voice. It says we *do* hear His voice! If we are His sheep, we have the ability to hear, follow, and understand what He's saying.

LEARN TO RECOGNIZE HIS VOICE

When I was a new believer, I heard people talk about how they "heard God" say this or that. I didn't know if they heard an audible voice from heaven or if they were on drugs. Either way, I felt shortchanged. Why couldn't I hear God speak to me?

Recognizing God's voice naturally occurs as your relationship with God develops. For example, if a new friend calls you on the telephone, chances are you may not recognize their voice the first time they call. As you spend more time with them, however, you'll begin to recognize their voice immediately. You may even have friends you haven't heard from in ten years, and when they call, you still recognize their voice. That is how God's voice is.

Once you recognize it, it becomes so familiar to you that you won't ever forget it.

GET RID OF INTERFERENCE

Many of us don't hear God's voice because we have too many distractions. Inappropriate relationships are one of the greatest interruptions that drown out the voice of God. In Abigail's case, it wasn't until Ethan broke it off with her that she realized what a distraction her relationship with him was to her relationship with God.

"As soon as he broke up with me, though, I was looking at other guys," she said. "I still wasn't divorced yet, and I'm thinking, *This is crazy. Something has to change.*"

Abigail continued: "I was in the break room at work and saw a flyer taped on the wall about a Bible study on Tuesday mornings. The first time I went, I felt like bawling the whole time, but these were people I worked with. I held it together until I got home that night, and then I just sobbed and sobbed. I wanted God back in my life. I didn't realize how far away I had pushed him."

For Abigail, her relationship with Ethan interfered with her relationship with God. Distractions, however, are not always "bad" things. Many times our lives are so crowded with good causes that we have no time to seek the Lord.

Michelle thought she was doing everything God wanted her to do. She home-schooled her two children, led a MOPS (Mothers of Preschoolers) group, diligently worked a home-based business to generate extra income, and faithfully obeyed financial guru Dave Ramsey's budget system. "By the end of the day, I was wiped out. I was trying so hard to please God, but the truth is I had no time for Him," she said.

Like too much salt can ruin a good meal, too many good activities can drown out our joy and defuse our ability to hear God. When we keep our lives free from clutter and distractions, we are in a better position to hear His voice.

TAKE A NAP

Sometimes it's the simple things that make the most sense. We can't clearly hear God's voice when we are full of anxiety. We're human and live in bodies that need rest. If our physical needs are deprived, they'll interfere with our ability to hear God. Sometimes the most spiritual thing we can do is sleep.

Casey learned that the hard way. After a bitter argument with her husband and no resolution in sight, she pressed even harder for some type of agreement. Casey had confused the command in Ephesians 4:26 to not to let the sun go down on your anger with the need to resolve a disagreement before going to sleep. Her demands for a resolution, however, only made things worse. By 2:00 A.M. she and Travis were both worn out and had to work the next day. Tensions flared and nasty exchanges were made. Finally Travis announced he was going to sleep.

Infuriated, Casey sobbed into her pillow and cried out to God, "If he loved me, he'd try to work this out tonight! Won't you make him roll over?"

Travis never budged. The next morning, however, Casey woke up with a different perspective. Her anguish subsided after getting some rest and the Lord spoke to her about her part in the disagreement. The night before, she was unable to hear God's voice because her body desperately needed rest. Weariness clogs our eyes and exaggerates issues. Now Casey realizes how weariness interferes with her ability to hear God's voice.

"If I can't hear God in a situation," she explains, "there's no way I can resolve a disagreement. I still need to forgive before I go to sleep, but the best thing I can do is get some rest and start fresh the next day."

WATCH YOUR CONFESSIONS

Our confessions are powerful. James 3:3-5 makes a strong case about the authority of the tongue. We can steer whole ships with a small rudder or control a horse with a tiny bit in his mouth. Like a rudder steers a ship or a bit controls a horse, words steer and control relationships. It's so easy to get it backward. Use your words to declare good things, not just report the bad things you see. God's Word instructs us to steer our life according to His will with the power of our tongue.

Negative confessions are the opposite of prayer. In fact, they deactivate prayer. When we pray and declare things that agree with God's will, our words go out into the heavenly realm to create. When we declare untruths and negative words, we nullify the power of prayer.

Joshua knew this from forty years of experience with the Israelites murmuring and complaining in the desert. After Moses died and Joshua was to lead the nation in the capture of Jericho, he knew he better put an end to their destructive words. That's why he issued a national decree. "Do not say a word until I give the sound" (Joshua 6:10). He knew their negative confessions had kept them out of the Promised Land for forty years, and he wasn't about to allow their mindless chatter to jeopardize the nation's victory any longer.

Murmuring is as contagious as gossiping. Ecclesiastes 4:12 says "a cord of three strands is not easily broken." This Scripture is usually quoted to show the power of agreement in prayer, but it works both ways. Individual murmurings are negative confessions. When we speak forth negative words and others begin to agree with us, they gain the strength of a snowball going down a mountain. As it gains momentum, it can start an avalanche.

Multiple agreements cause our words of doubt to bear more strength. Jesus tells us in Matthew 18:19 that if two of us on earth agree about anything they ask for, it will be done. Jesus didn't say this only works for positive confessions. It works both ways, negative and positive.

Murmuring is like spreading poison to others. Since it's impossible to keep it all inside, not only does it keep us in bondage, it seeps out and affects those around us. When you're tempted to complain, ask God to help you zip your lip. When you keep a guard on your lips, you can steer your soul-health and relationships in a totally new direction.

If you have trouble discerning God's voice, don't be discouraged. The more time you spend with God, the easier it gets to recognize His voice and trust your gut. To help you with that, the next chapter has simple, yet effective resources and Scriptures to strengthen your prayer life. In the meantime, use the six suggestions you just learned to position yourself so you're more likely to hear His voice and trust your inner witness.

-17-

Strengthening Your Prayer Life

A SOUL-HEALTHY WOMAN understands the power of prayer and spends time daily talking to God. She knows the benefits of peace and the ability to receive divine direction are essential to living in freedom. She may be wise in her own eyes, but knows her own intellect is no match for the wisdom of God. He gives us wisdom she could never find elsewhere. Plus, when she adds prayer to the other steps to breaking the toxic love cycle it produces a multiplier effect.

PRAYER SCRIPTURE TRUTHS

+ "Do not be anxious about anything, but in every-thing, by prayer and petition, with thanksgiving, present your requests to God. And the peace of God, which transcends all understanding, will guard your hearts and your minds in Christ Jesus" (Philippians 4:6-7).

◆ "Call to me and I will answer you and tell you great and unsearchable things you do not know" (Jeremiah 33:3).

◆ "If any of you lacks wisdom, he should ask God, who gives generously to all without finding fault, and it will be given to him" (James 1:5).

◆ "For the eyes of the Lord are on the righteous and his ears are attentive to their prayer, but the face of the Lord is against those who do evil" (1 Peter 3:12).

◆ "And this is my prayer: that your love may abound more and more in knowledge and depth of insight, so that you may be able to discern what is best and may be pure and blameless for the day of Christ" (Philippians 1:9-10).

◆ "Again, I tell you that if two of you on earth agree about anything you ask for, it will be done for you by my Father in heaven. For where two or three come together in my name, there am I with them" (Matthew 18:19).

◆ "You want something but don't get it. You kill and covet, but you cannot have what you want. You quarrel and fight. You do not have, because you do not ask God. When you ask, you do not receive, because you ask with wrong motives, that you may spend what you get on your pleasures" (James 4:2-3).

PRAYER ACTION POINTS

Remember, prayer is the practice of conversing with God to seek direction and wisdom. To strengthen your habit of prayer, try the following action points to boost your ability to hear God's voice.

Listen Intentionally

Want to grow your faith? Listen to something inspiring. Romans 10:17 says that our faith comes from hearing the Word of God, so make time to listen.

The average person spends one to three hours a day in their car. Use this down time to listen to a Christian radio program or an inspiring audio message. If your church sells audio messages of sermons, purchase them and keep them in your car so when you have time to listen, you'll have something uplifting to build your faith. Check your church bookstore for messages on sale. Many churches offer deep discounts on older messages. Purchase audio messages on CD from your favorite pastors or speakers. You can also check out audio books from your local library.

The car isn't the only place we have down time. If you like to work out, you can upload messages to your iPod and work out your spirit and body at the same time.

Watch Something Inspiring

The selection of Christian programming on cable television has dramatically increased over the last several years. Record your favorite programs so you can watch at your convenience. There's an even larger selection of programs available online. You can literally choose your subject matter, sermon topic, or favorite verse.

Read Your Bible

Set aside at least five or ten minutes a day to allow God to speak to you through His Word. If you don't know where to start, search online to find a daily reading plan or purchase a one-year Bible that breaks down reading into daily segments. Many Christian websites also offer daily Scriptures or inspiring thoughts through email or text messages.

Your local Christian bookstore also has a large selection of Christian books suitable for challenging your faith and keeping your prayer life focused on God's Word. If you'd rather shop online, Amazon offers discounts on many books. If you travel frequently, consider buying an electronic reader like a Kindle or Nook. Don't forget to stock up on digital books.

Bible studies are also a great way to enhance your prayer habit. Studying with a group that is reading through the same material can be very enlightening as well as provide for much needed fellowship and encouragement from other believers. You also have opportunities to pray for others and have them pray for you, too.

Find a Prayer Partner

Enlist a girlfriend you trust to pray regularly with you. You can meet for coffee and exchange prayer requests or simply have a prayer connection over the phone. Either way, the power of agreement is a huge faith builder. Having someone to share your burdens and joys with is spiritually strengthening. When difficulties come, you have someone to encourage you, and when prayers are answered, you have someone to rejoice with.

I purposely mentioned having a *female* prayer partner. The spiritual connection that comes from sharing prayer requests can be quite intimate and can influence a love junkie's discernment about the direction of a relationship. Whether you are married or single, exercise wisdom and connect with a female prayer partner. In addition, if you are dating someone, I'd like to offer a word of caution about praying alone together too soon in relationship. It's perfectly acceptable to pray in a group setting. In fact, you'll want to do that so you can evaluate a potential partner's Christian walk, but praying alone together should be reserved for later in the relationship to avoid a counterfeit oneness, which the intimacy of prayer can create. I urge you to evaluate the character and relationship suitability of a dating partner before you allow the bonds of prayer to bind you to someone who may not be marriage material.

Attend Church Regularly

Hebrews 10:25 tells us not to give up meeting together because it's in the "meeting together" that we are able to encourage one another. Make it a habit to attend worship experiences consistently. You'll not only have the opportunity to worship through song and listen to God's Word, but you'll also build relationships with like-minded people.

Listen to Praise Music

I can't tell you how often I've heard God speak to me through a song. Music is a language all its own and has a way of communicating what words can't. Music lifts my spirit and ministers to my soul. When we sing songs of praise to God, we edify Him.

Psalm 69:30-31 says that it pleases God when we praise His name in song and glorify Him in thanksgiving.

Establish a Regular Devotional Time

Start your morning off with a devotional. Buy a devotional book or sign up for one to be sent to your email or phone. Throughout the day, meditate and reflect on the truth that you started your day with. Often you may even notice a theme of what God is saying to you personally. A verse may jump out at you during your devotional, and then later that day, you'll hear it on the radio, see it in an email or notice it in a book you're reading. I'm always amazed when God does this with me. It shows that if we listen, we can hear His voice. Most devotionals include a short prayer with each entry. By all means, pray that prayer, but don't stop there. Continue your own conversation with God, centered around the theme of the day.

Memorize Scripture

Learning verses by memory is a way to meditate on God's Word and massage its truth deep into your spirit. You won't find the word *memorize* in the Bible, but we are instructed many times to remember. My favorite verse encouraging us to remember is Psalm 143:5: "I remember the days of long ago; I meditate on all your works and consider what your hands have done."

Pick verses that minister to you about prayer, and make it a point to meditate on them and memorize them. When you commit God's Word to memory, it's stored in the recesses of your mind, and when you need it the most, it will come flooding back to minister to you. Memorizing Scripture can reinforce God's truth in your heart. When challenges arise, you'll be more in-clined to declare and agree with God's truth rather than spout negative confessions.

Keep a Prayer Journal

Journaling is easy. All you need is a pen and a notebook. Write down the date and record your prayers. These prayers can either be you speaking to God or a record of what you think God is saying to you. I especially believe it's important to write down vague thoughts, dreams, or visions. If you're not sure whether what you're hearing is your own voice or the voice of God, take time to pause, reflect, and wait. But if you don't write it down when it's fresh on your mind, you'll probably forget it.

Later, you can go back, review your thoughts and prayers and see if any of your circumstances have brought clarity or confir-mation. It's hard to deny that God has spoken something to you when you see proof in your own writing after it has come to pass. It will cement your faith and convince you that you indeed hear His voice.

QUESTIONS TO PONDER

1. How would you describe your prayer life?

   ❏ "Non-existent."

   ❏ "A rant session. I feel much better after I scream and holler."

   ❏ "It's more of a lecture. God is the professor. I just listen and learn."

❏ "Like a text message. We talk daily, but it's short and sweet."

❏ "It's a friends-and-family plan. I have God on speed dial with unlimited access."

2. Think about the times you've heard God's voice or felt His presence. Where were you or what were you doing? How might positioning yourself back in that environment aid you in hearing God's voice more frequently?

3. Read Philippians 4:6-7. What does it mean to guard your heart? In romantic relationships, do you tend to overprotect or underprotect your heart?

4. According to Matthew 18:19, if two on earth agree about anything, it will be done in heaven. If we declare something contrary to God's Word, and others agree with our negative confessions, how might they deactivate our prayers?

5. Ecclesiastes 4:12 says a cord of three strands is not easily broken. Bible teachers call this principle the power of agreement in prayer. Psychologists call it the Pygmalion effect or a self-fulfilling prophecy. Describe a time when you witnessed this truth in action with either gossip and murmuring or praise and affirmation.

6. Sometimes we get so busy that we set aside our prayer time. What types of distractions most often interfere with your prayer time or ability to hear God's voice?

7. In Genesis 37, Joseph had a dream at the age of seventeen. Between his dream and destiny, he experienced over two decades of hardships that prepared him for his future. How does knowing that God used Joseph's desert season to prepare him for his destiny encourage you to believe for your own dream?

The step of embracing an active prayer life is crucial to recovery from relationship addiction because most love junkies have discounted their inner witness. As a result, they have often accepted unacceptable relationships. With a healthy prayer life to gain discernment, however, you can learn how to pay attention to your instinct, hear the voice of God and position yourself to make healthy relationship choices.

–18–

STEP NUMBER 5:
Resolve

RESOLVE: THE PRACTICE OF ADDING DIVINE
REVELATION TO MY HUMAN STRENGTH.

WHEN IT COMES TO ROMANCE, worldly wisdom tells us to listen to our heart. Over and over we hear well-meaning friends and family advise: "Just follow your heart." This common advice, however, contradicts Scripture. Jeremiah 17:9 says, "No one can understand or know the heart. It is deceitful and beyond cure."

Listening to the voice or witness of God within our heart is different than listening to our own understanding. Our own heart is the seat of our emotions and passions and contains our own desires, but God's witness to our heart contains His desires. He communicates His will to our heart, but it's often different from our own selfish ambitions. Add to this contrast the fact that our willpower alone is often insufficient to comply with God's commands. That's why so many of us continue to make the same mistakes over and over. That's why a revelation is essential to overcome areas where we've previously struggled. Tara's story explains what I mean.

INTENTIONAL DEFENSE

Tara's dark locks fell around her face as John and I listened to her story. She brushed errant strands aside and let out a sigh of disappointment. "I never thought I'd do something like this. I don't even know if I'm saved," she began. "How can I be a Christian and sleep with a married man?"

Tara loved the Lord and she desperately wanted to honor His Word, but there was a weakness in her life that compromised her will. On the outside, it seemed like she made all the right choices. She willed to live a pure life and promised to save herself for her husband, but countless times she fell into moral compromise. Unfortunately, Tara is not a rare example. Many Christian women struggle with sexual sin.

Willpower alone is insufficient to stand up against temptation. That's why so many women fail when faced with situations where passion is stretched to the limits.

Tara leaned back in her chair and took a sip of water. "I have good boundaries. I can tell a guy 'no' over and over. My first line of defense is strong," she admitted, "but once that is broken, I'm weak."

Knowing Tara loved sports, my husband used a football analogy to help her understand how the enemy slipped past her defense.

"When the quarterback snaps the ball and hands it off to his running back," John began, "the running back looks for a hole in the defensive line. Once he breaks through this first line of defense, there aren't as many players in the backfield to defend against the run. Once he breaks through that first line of defense, his chances of scoring a touchdown are much greater. Tara, you're like a team with a weak defense."

Like a football coach examines areas of weakness in his team to discover where the opposition is able to penetrate his line of defense, we began to discuss ways in which the enemy was able to penetrate Tara's will. We talked about her motives and areas of vulnerability.

Tara knew my background and how my own will used to be weak because of my need for affection and affirmation.

"Those aren't triggers for me," explained Tara. "I don't think my need for attention or loneliness causes me to sleep with guys. I grew up with a great family. We are still close today. I know this sounds bad, but I think I compromise my will out of sheer boredom. I come home from work, I'm tired, and Eric calls. I've told him he can't come over countless times, but one day he insisted on bringing breakfast over. I was bored, and the next thing I know, I finally said okay. He came over and one hug was all it took. *Bam!* The next thing I know we're in bed together."

"Let's talk about your boredom," I said. "I think you've hit on something there."

"I honestly live the most boring life imaginable."

"What do you like to do in your free time?" I asked.

"I don't really have any hobbies. In high school, I played competitive sports. Nothing has ever replaced that."

Bingo!

We found a spot where Tara was unprotected. If the enemy could penetrate past her first line of defense, he could sneak past her boredom and score every time. (Sorry, no pun intended.)

Now that Tara identified her weakness, we talked about ways she could guard her will by covering her boredom with activity. When we're busy, we aren't easily distracted. It's when we're alone and isolated that the enemy attacks.

"I feel like a twelve-year-old kid telling my mom, 'I'm bored,'" said Tara. "It sounds so silly to admit, but I really think that's why I fall into sin."

After Tara left that day, I poured over Scriptures to find evidence in the Word that boredom makes us vulnerable to sin and temptation. It took a while, however, because the word boredom is not in the Bible. What our culture refers to as boredom, the Bible calls *idleness*.

You may have heard the saying, "Idleness is the devil's workshop." It's not a scripture, but it's a righteous principle. We're supposed to warn those who are idle (1 Thessalonians 5:14), shun the bread of idleness (Proverbs 31:27), and if we're lazy, we won't get the promise (Hebrews 6:12).

Idleness comes from the Greek word *shiphluwth* which means inactivity, slothfulness, sluggishness, remissness. When we are remiss, we are negligent, careless, lacking force or energy. Does that sound like boredom or what?

When we're inactive, boredom and laziness set in and we become easy prey for the enemy. When we're idle, our will is weakened. We fall into the trap of thinking there's nothing better to do. When we're busy and preoccupied, it's easier to say no.

I told Tara to make a list of activities she enjoys. She would have to develop the discipline to engage in them. This would be her way of protecting her weakness and putting a guard in place—or a second line of defense—to protect her areas of vulnerability. She would have to be intentional about her defense.

WHY WILLPOWER ALONE
IS INSUFFICIENT

Webster's Dictionary defines willpower as "the ability to control one's impulses and actions, self-control." In other words, our ability to control our will is based on the power of our individual decision and strength. In Tara's case, her willpower or restraint was limited. I don't think she's alone.

If it's not empowered by divine vision, our restraint or human strength alone will fail every time. Even Scripture agrees with this premise. Proverbs 29:18 says, "Where there is no revelation, the people cast off restraint; but blessed is he who keeps the law."

Basically, a lack of revelation produces a lack of restraint. If we break this truth down into an equation, it would look like this:

Zero Revelation = Zero Restraint

On the other hand, if someone who has revelation and restraint is someone who keeps the law, then our equation would look like this:

Revelation + Restraint (Willpower) = Someone who Keeps the Law (someone who has resolve)

If we reduce the equation to its simplest form, we would have:

Revelation + Willpower = Resolve

As you can see from this equation, resolve includes willpower, but is much stronger than willpower alone because it includes the strength of a divine revelation.

That's what was wrong with Tara's ability to resist. She was attempting to make her resolve effective with only the power of her will. That strategy may work for a while or work for things that are not overly tempting. As individuals, however, all of us have areas of weakness. Our resolve may be strong in the area of managing our money, but weak in the area of anger management. Or we may have great resolve in the area of reading our Bible, but weak in the area of choosing likeminded companions.

Here's the bottom line: The strength of your resolve will never be greater than your revelation. So what can you do if you don't have a revelation? Get one! While you can't force a revelation, you can position yourself in such a way that getting a clear understanding of God's Word is more likely. You can do this with what I call a MAP, my acronym for meditate, ask, and point.

MEDITATE

Earlier we talked about how the word *meditate* comes from the Hebrew word *hagah,* which means to mutter. Contrary to cultural influences that portray mediation as a silent activity, biblical meditating is not a quiet function. When we meditate on Scripture or God's truth, we are literally thinking out loud. But it's a disciplined style of thinking. We don't let our thoughts ramble or our mind wander. Instead we target our thoughts in a divine direction; we mutter and declare God's Word. We pray and reflect. We speak His truth and listen for answers. And then something awesome happens. Our meditation sets the stage for revelation. Our faith is increased as we hear ourselves release truth into the atmosphere.

Why is revelation so important? Because Satan knows our weaknesses better than we do. One of the best ways to increase our revelation is to meditate on God's truth. As you read God's Word, pay attention to Scriptures that seem to prick your heart. Write them down. Think about them. Say them out loud. Contemplate their meaning.

Look up verses that deal with specific subjects that God is stirring in your heart. As you meditate and think on these truths, you create an atmosphere for revelation to occur. The more you meditate, the more likely it is that you'll get a revelation.

ASK

When my family went on vacation to San Francisco, we took a tour of Grace Cathedral, one of the largest Gothic-style cathedrals in the United States. In the outdoor courtyard of the church was a prayer labyrinth—a circular maze used as an instrument to facilitate meditation, prayer, and personal reflection. The labyrinth outlines a walking path for a prayer journey. The guided path helps the person on the prayer walk stay focused. They begin the walk with a question or prayer concern. As they walk the maze, they listen, meditate, ponder, and pray. The goal is to receive an answer by the time they get to the center part of the circular maze. On the return walk, they find empowerment to apply what they've heard.

Walking and praying brings our prayers alive. Meditating also causes us to pay more attention to our thoughts. Speaking our thoughts out loud causes us to notice when we declare things that contradict God's Word.

Why is it so important that our words agree with God's words? Hebrews 4:12 says that the Word of God is alive and powerful, sharper than any two-edged sword. Isaiah 55:11 advises that God's Word will not return empty, but will achieve the purpose for which it was sent. Obviously, God's Word is a powerful weapon, but check out what the book of Numbers says about the words we mutter. It's a huge responsibility to make sure our words agree with Scriptures.

"I will do the very thing I've heard you say" (Numbers 14:28).

Be careful what you ask for.

Our prayers are like ordering at a restaurant. When you go to a restaurant, the waiter places an order based on what you ask for. They ask what you want, deliver your order to the kitchen, and bring what you order to your table. They don't bring you a hamburger if you ordered a chicken salad. In the same way, when we release our prayer requests to heaven, the Holy Spirit is released to "take our order." So make sure your words "order" what you want to receive. Ask and you shall receive.

POINT

The book of Daniel tells the story of how Daniel was taken captive and deported to Babylon. There he was immersed in a prayerless society characterized by idol worship and overindulgence. Sound familiar? Even though he was surrounded by an ungodly culture, however, Daniel remained determined to follow God. He prayed even though it violated the law. He worshipped God even under the threat of death. But Daniel took his devotion one step further. He also resolved not to defile himself with the royal food and wine (Daniel 1:8).

What gave Daniel the ability to resist foods that everyone else ate? What gave him the power to turn down things that everyone else enjoyed? How did he get the endurance to abstain from the indulgences and pleasures the world celebrated?

I don't believe Daniel's efforts were entirely his own. He wasn't a superhero. He was human just like us. But somehow he was able to tap into a supernatural strength that empowered his will.

In Daniel 1:8, the King James Version uses the word *purposed* instead of *resolve*. Purposed comes from the Hebrew word *suwm,* which means to ordain or to establish, to set in such a way that the enemy cannot penetrate; to construct a nest habitation in a rock, to create a stronghold.

Daniel's resolve, or purpose, was so much stronger than a mere decision. It was a decision protected by a stronghold—a place impenetrable by the enemy, a fortress in time of attack. He purposed in his heart to surrender his own desires to God's will. He was empowered by conviction and took dominion over his beliefs, casting aside his own wishes.

Not only did he abstain from food, but he refused to cower in defeat even when his life was threatened by execution (Daniel 2:12), by fire (Daniel 3:17), and by torture in the lion's den (Daniel 6:7). When Daniel was surrounded by the enemy, he begged God for revelation. And God answered him.

During the night, a mystery was revealed to Daniel in a vision (Daniel 2:19). I don't think that was the first time Daniel had a vision. Daniel had a habit of visiting with God and he expected Him to answer. God reveals His secrets to those who have a habit of seeking Him. Going to God for vision was Daniel's fortress. He didn't rely on his own wisdom. He knew his only power against the enemy was a revelation. Like Daniel, a revelation can give us the strength to conquer wavering opinions and doubts. Divine vision can equip us to stand up against the enemy's attacks and defeat the powers of darkness.

Before I had a revelation, I failed miserably in my ability to resist sexual temptations. I'd decide over and over that I would stay pure, but countless times my own willpower proved inadequate. I needed a revelation to empower my resolve. Thankfully, I finally found the secret that enabled me to conquer sexual temptations. Are you curious? That's what I'd like to share with you next.

—19—

Why Say "No" to Sex?

" 'FORNICATION' SOUNDS LIKE SUCH A STALE
ARCHAIC WORD THAT OUR GENERATION DOESN'T
EVEN KNOW WHAT IT MEANS. IT SOUNDS OUTDATED.
BUT THIS IS THE GENIUS OF MASS MARKETING.
SEX SELLS . . . SEX SELLS CLOTHES, IT SELLS
MOVIES, IT SELLS MAGAZINES, IT SELLS EVERYTHING.
OUR PRESENT ATTITUDE TOWARD SEX IS
THE RESULT OF MASS MARKETING."
—DAVID MACDONALD

YOU MAY HAVE HEARD IT BEFORE—sex outside of marriage is wrong. But why? And what is it about the covenant of marriage that makes sex permissive all of a sudden?

Even though the advertising industry uses sex to sell everything from toothpaste to tennis shoes, most of us know sex is supposed to be reserved for marriage. For me, sex was a big "Shall Not." *Thou shall not have sex before marriage.* But why? Honestly, I had no clue.

I couldn't even find the word *sex* in the Bible. Warnings about promiscuity were concealed in words popular decades ago—fornication, lasciviousness, and debauchery, further adding to the mystery about why sex was forbidden before marriage. Even so, because I loved God, I strived to honor His Word, but without a revelation, my resolve faded.

It wasn't long after John and I started dating that we began sleeping together. I knew it was wrong, but my willpower was no match for my weakness. I've never done well following rules without reason, and I'd never heard anyone give a good reason to abstain from sex. I was doomed to fail. If I had been born in another century, I'd have a large capital "A" branded on my chest or would've been burned at the stake to atone for my sin of adultery.

After John proposed, however, the conviction to obey God's Word grew even stronger. One day, in desperation, I cried out to God, "If you want me to obey, Lord, I need to know why!"

Well, guess what? He answered.

"I have a blessing to give your marriage, and the only way you can receive it is to abstain."

A blessing?

That was news to me. In fact, it was a huge revelation. I had never heard anyone talk about a blessing for abstinence. All of a sudden, a regulation transformed into a revelation. I felt empowered to deny my flesh because I wanted the blessing. There was a prize for obedience.

THE PRIZE IS BETTER THAN SEX

I told John about my conviction and at first he hesitated slightly. "No sex? Are you sure?" His flesh put up a hissy fit, but soon he was on board. He wanted the blessing too.

We asked God for forgiveness and asked for His strength. I'm convinced our resolve would not have been possible without repentance. Through the last seven months of our courtship, John and I abstained from sex. We embraced my MAP concept: meditate, ask, and point. It worked for us. We meditated on God's truth. We asked for God's perspective, and we pointed our eyes toward the goal. We didn't know what the prize was, but we knew it must be something great if it was better than the sex we had to forsake. God doesn't withhold things from us to be mean. He withholds things to give us something better.

In his book *Choosing God's Best*, Dr. Don Raunikar writes, "Obedience is how we show God we love Him, and the obedience must always come before understanding."[21]

It wasn't easy, but God showed us ways to protect our decision. He gave us boundaries—like not being alone together after midnight. The Lord revealed to John that willpower fades dramatically after the clock strikes midnight. He also instructed John that as the future spiritual leader of our family, he was to take the lead in developing our prayer life as a couple. And the most essential boundary of all was this: When passions rage, pray immediately. To be sure, nothing puts out the flame of passion quite like prayer. Prayer is an instantaneous redirect.

By the time we got married on January 1, 1999, our relationship was stronger than I could ever have imagined. We had done it God's way. Abstaining from sex gave us time to develop other areas of our relationship that were essential to laying a strong foundation for marriage. Instead of allowing lust to interfere with God's plan for our marriage, we were free to develop the emotional and spiritual areas of our relationship—areas that no doubt would have been neglected had we continued to indulge in the physical relationship prematurely.

Many Christian marriages begin with a thriving sexual relationship and a weak spiritual relationship. This is the opposite of God's intent. Dr. Raunikar discusses counterfeit oneness in his book. He writes: "The dangers and complications of premarital sex intensify when each person thinks their situation is different—that somehow being in love has made everything okay. I have couples who come to me searching for God's will in their relationship and yet they are sexually involved. Scripture clearly says they are living outside the will of God. Their own unrepented sin will put a plug in their communication line with God (Isaiah 59:1-2)."

During our courtship, John and I spent considerable time praying together, something I know we wouldn't have made a priority without the commitment to abstain. Often, God confirmed His Word to us as a couple and synchronized our visions. These confirmations created a powerful base from which to build our marriage. They cemented our faith when times of adversity came.

Revelation empowers us to follow *all* the words of His law (Deuteronomy 29:29).

> *Many Christian marriages begin with a thriving sexual relationship and a weak spiritual relationship.*

CHEMISTRY . . . FACT OR FICTION?

"I met Ben in my Economics class my freshman year of college," said Dadriane. "At first I wasn't interested, but he wouldn't stop texting me. He left notes on my car and even copied assignments for me when I missed class. I told him no several times when he asked me out, but in a weak moment, I finally said yes. He was serious about his studies and seemed even more serious about me. After a couple of weeks, we were alone at his apartment when he pressured me to have sex. I relented. Then as quickly as he pursued me, he vanished. It's crazy because I really wasn't attracted to him in the first place, but after we had sex, I was convinced we had something special. I tried to call him several times, but he totally brushed me off. I was devastated. How can guys turn off their interest so quickly?"

Science has an answer for this: oxytocin. Oxytocin is a hormone released in females during childbirth and post-delivery during lactation and the milk let-down phase. Oxytocin is a natural hormone released to allow the mother and baby to bond. Interestingly, it is also released during an orgasm. Often referred to as the love hormone, oxytocin facilitates emotional bonding, explaining why a sexual encounter intensifies the union.

Especially in women.

While oxytocin affects both men and women, it doesn't affect them both in the same degree. In women, the effects are amplified by estrogen and increase with each successive orgasm. For men, the effects can be short lived. In fact, testosterone can counteract the effects. This explains the often common occurrence after casual sex where the woman wants to cuddle and the man is ready to bolt. It may also explain the story of Amnon and Tamar in 2 Samuel 13. Amnon was so obsessed with Tamar to the point that he literally got sick, so he devised a scheme to seduce her. When she refused his advances, he raped her, but as soon as he was through with her, he hated her more than he ever loved her.

Notoriously dubbed the cuddle drug, oxytocin is also released through touch. Even thinking of someone we want to be with can stimulate this hormone. The hormonal response oxytocin provides explains why so many women are unable to walk away from men they "know" they shouldn't be involved with. When you have sex with someone, all of a sudden this hormone kicks in and bonds you together like Gorilla Glue. Whether he is a wise choice for you or not, you suddenly experience an irresistible connection you can't control. No wonder women are confused.

THE AFFECTION CONNECTION

We don't have to be sleeping with a man to be under the influence of oxytocin. Merely being aroused by holding hands, touching, and kissing can cause us to fall under its spell. The effects of oxytocin can be addictive, causing us to want more. The more we are touched, the more our oxytocin levels rise, and the more we crave to be touched again.

Oxytocin can also decrease our mental faculties and impair our memory. It's why touching our partner during an argument can still the storm. It's also why make-up sex so often glosses over a passionate argument.

"It happened every time," said Amy. "Steve and I argued constantly about the bills. Ever since he moved in, he promised to pay his fair share, but he was always short. He spent all his money on clothing. 'Gotta look good for my clients,' he'd say. His vanity sickened me. I threatened countless times to end the relationship, but every time, he'd give me this *look*. Then he'd circle in like I was his prey. I don't know how, but it worked like a charm. I feel so stupid. We'd have the best sex, and afterwards, I'd forget why I was so mad."

AVOIDING SEDUCTION

Carrie Underwood's popular song *Cowboy Casanova* makes light of this phenomenon, but it appears there's more truth to her words than we realize. The lyrics liken the man to a curse and a drug, someone who can create addiction for those who fall for him.

We know better, we just don't know how to get off the merry-go-round. Oxytocin is an intravenous secret love sauce with mind-altering ramifications. If oxytocin is released through simple touch, how can we avoid the seduction of this devious drug? The answer sounds outdated in today's sexually tolerant culture, but the only way to completely avoid the hormone's influence is to not even allow our passions to be aroused or awakened in the first place.

Scripture warns against promiscuity and sexual intercourse before marriage, but the Bible actually holds us to an even higher standard. Scripture doesn't just advise against intercourse, but advises against the mere arousal of our passion. "Do not arouse or awaken love until it so desires" (Song of Solomon 8:4). I challenge you to consider this Scripture an answer to the question, "How far is too far?" Most of us crave relationship. We want to be united with another person who will love and cherish us. If we try to obtain this outside of God's will, however, we create a mess, putting ourselves smack dab in the middle of compromise. The findings about oxytocin provide powerful evidence of why we should be committed to following God's laws about sexual arousal. The only way to stay safe is to be in the center of obedience. Oxytocin is intended to bond husband and wife *after* marriage.

IS IT LUST OR LOVE?

We have a false sense of confidence when we think we can control lust. Lust is like a beast with a strong appetite that cannot be tamed. There's a delicate point of no return when it can no longer be contained. The only way to control it is by prevention.

Lust is like a fire. In certain environments fire is extremely beneficial. It creates warmth and enables us to cook. It has benefits to artists who are able to melt gold and design jewelry. Under the wrong circumstances, however, it's dangerous and harmful. When the fire is not controlled, it can destroy whole cities and take lives.

Desire is also like a fire. In the right environment, it has many benefits. It is comforting and adds much pleasure in marriage, but outside of God's intended use for passion, it is as destructive as a wild fire. Once ignited, it's almost impossible to contain.

One of the best ways to protect your heart is to resist sexual temptations and say "no" to sex before marriage—and yet, this is one of the most difficult habits to apply. If you struggle with maintaining your sexual integrity, however, don't lose heart. You can fortify your resolve if you are willing. A revelation about your sexual integrity is vital to empowering your resolve.

–20–

Strengthening Your Resolve

A REVELATION IS THE KEY to maintaining your resolve and sexual integrity because a divine revelation empowers your willpower. Your human strength alone is no match for the temptations your flesh fights, and while you can't create a revelation, you can position yourself in such a way that you are more likely to hear from God and receive one. In the meantime, the following Scriptures and action points will help you set boundaries in place to protect your flesh from temptation.

RESOLVE SCRIPTURE TRUTHS

+ "Where there is no revelation, the people cast off restraint; but blessed is he who keeps the law" (Proverbs 29:18).

+ "Therefore, prepare your minds for action; be self-controlled; set your hope fully on the grace to be given you when Jesus Christ is revealed. As obedient children, do not conform to the evil desires you had when you lived in ignorance. But just as he who called you is holy, so be holy in all you do" (1 Peter 1:13-15).

+ "Do not conform any longer to the pattern of this world, but be transformed by the renewing of your mind. Then you will be able to test and approve what God's will is—his good, pleasing and perfect will" (Romans 12:2).

+ "He who doubts is like a wave of the sea, blown and tossed by the wind. That man should not think he will receive anything from the Lord; he is a double-minded man, unstable in all he does" (James 1:6-8).

+ "Watch and pray so that you will not fall into temptation. The spirit is willing, but the body is weak" (Matthew 26:41).

+ "She watches over the affairs of her household and does not eat the bread of idleness" (Proverbs 31:27)

+ "And we urge you, brothers, warn those who are idle and disruptive, encourage the timid, help the weak, be patient with everyone" (1 Thessalonians 5:14).

+ "If a man is lazy, the rafters sag; if his hands are idle, the house leaks" (Ecclesiastes 10:18).

+ "So we fix our eyes not on what is seen, but on what is unseen. For what is seen is temporary, but what is unseen is eternal" (2 Corinthians 4:18).

RESOLVE ACTION POINTS

Remember, resolve is the practice of adding divine revelation to our human strength. If you have trouble with the habit of resolve, try the following action points to strengthen your resolve.

Pray for Revelation

It's so much easier to have resolve when our focus is based on a revelation rather than our own determination. If you need more revelation, find a place where you are not distracted. A calm environment makes it easier to hear from God. Take some time to pray and ask Him to empower you with renewed vision. Use the MAP acronym for *meditate, ask,* and *point* to position yourself in a place where you're more likely to receive divine direction.

Create a Plan

Just like we practice fire drills and tornado drills to prepare ahead for a time of emergency, we have to know ahead of time what we will do in the event of temptation or disaster. Create a detailed emergency plan to put into action when you're faced with temptation. Write down your "stop, drop, and roll" plan. Then follow through.

Find a Focal Point

Find a focal point, a Scripture, an encouraging thought, or a place of focus that you can concentrate on to break the vicious cycle. A focal point in times of temptation draws our attention back to our resolve. If we don't surrender to temptation, eventually it passes.

Establish Boundaries

Put effective boundaries in place. List ways you can avoid people, places, and things that cause you to compromise. If you have trouble with boundaries, have a trusted friend help you brainstorm ideas.

Fill Your Schedule

Relaxation is fine in moderation, but when you have too much free time in your schedule, you are setting yourself up for a fall. It's perfectly acceptable to have free time to watch television, flip through magazines, or surf the internet, but that time should be designated as time to chill, so in reality, you *are* doing something—relaxing. It's when your rest and relaxation time is excessive that boredom sets in, so be careful to exercise moderation.

If you spend too much time on unfocused activities, reevaluate your schedule and commit yourself to purposeful activities. You might consider exercising, volunteering for a church or non-profit group, or taking a class to further your education. Purpose protects vulnerability. That's because Satan leaves us alone when we are strong. He waits patiently for an opportune time, so don't give the enemy an opportunity to strike.

HALT

Our greatest temptations come when we are most vulnerable. Use the acronym HALT to remind yourself not to make decisions when you're *hungry, angry, lonely,* or *tired.* Postpone decisions until you have a chance to get refreshed. Satan waited to tempt Jesus until Jesus was hungry, lonely, and tired in the desert, and he does the same with us. He always waits for an opportune time (Luke 4:13). Don't give him one.

Go on a Fast

Even though a fast is abstaining from food, it does wonders to refresh our inner man. Fasting unclogs spiritual distractions and helps renew our perspective. It also detoxes us from the impurities that can block our ability to hear God's voice. If fasting from food is not a safe option for you, you may try abstaining from activities you enjoy or give up a certain type of food for a period of time.

Confess Your Sins

Find a trustworthy friend with whom you can share your struggle and who will pray with you. Sin breeds in darkness, but when it is brought into the light, God purifies us from the struggle of sin. Keeping sins hidden in darkness makes it easier for us to justify our behavior and become even more entrapped.

Write Down Your Goals

Set written and measurable goals and share them with a trusted friend who will follow up with you. Putting your goals on paper helps you maintain focus. Sharing them with a friend helps enforce accountability.

QUESTIONS TO PONDER

1. Which of the following areas trigger compromise for you?

     a. The need for approval and validation
     b. The need for affection
     c. Lustful thoughts
     d. The desire for purpose
     e. Loneliness
     f. Boredom
     g. The desire for companionship

2. What can you do to increase your revelation in those areas?

3. Boundaries are like an intentional defense system. What can you do to increase your boundaries or restraints to guard against compromise in those areas?

4. Our hearts are deceitful (Jeremiah 17:9). How can the desires of your heart lead you astray?

5. Have you ever fallen into sin because you were bored or idle? How can you prevent a reoccurrence?

6. How much do you think your own romantic tendencies are influenced by the hormone oxytocin? What makes you more vulnerable to its effects?

When you position yourself to get a revelation and begin to grow in the knowledge of God's will, He adds power to your will. With this divine understanding, you'll have the fortitude to refuse things that once restrained you.

Of course, there will always be times when we need the wisdom and insight of others. We would do well to give others the authority to speak into our life and help guard our areas of vulnerability. We are wise when we submit our lives to the counsel of others, which leads to the next step for soul-healthy women—the habit of embracing accountability.

-21-

STEP NUMBER 6:
Accountability

ACCOUNTABILITY: THE PRACTICE OF
PROTECTING MY WILL BY SURRENDERING
MY CHOICES TO WISE COUNSEL.

WE ALL HAVE BLIND SPOTS. When I'm driving, I
have to look over my shoulder before switching lanes. Without
a rearview mirror and side windows, I may crash and burn. We
have blind spots when it comes to love, too. Too many women
assume that everything a potential love interest says is certified
truth, but everyone puts their best foot forward in the beginning
of a relationship.

That's why it is important to complete an inspection.
Evaluating character takes time, but one thing is certain: the
truth comes out eventually. To avoid the crash and burn of an
unhealthy relationship, take things slow when you are getting to
know a guy, and align yourself with wise counsel. An accountability partner can help reveal your blind spots and keep you
from potential heartbreak.

PROCEED WITH CAUTION

Not all Christians are purebreds. Some are "Chreathens"—part Christian, part heathen (i.e. they may be saved, but their lifestyle might still be very worldly). Amanda met Wayne at church in a small-group recovery program. Although he seemed charming and sincere, he had just been released from prison for a drug offense. Instead of rushing into a relationship with Wayne, Amanda observed his behavior over time in a group setting. Although she was eager to go out with him, she wanted to proceed with caution. A few months later, when Amanda discovered Wayne had gone back to dealing drugs, she was glad she hadn't rushed into things.

A revelation about her previous relationship weaknesses motivated Amanda to take it slow. When we aren't emotionally attached, it's easier to notice areas of concern and potential character flaws. Character is like underwear: You hope the person you're with has some on, but the only time you know for sure is when you see them in a compromising position.

"In the past, I wouldn't have noticed the red flags," Amanda admitted. "But this time I did. Some of his behavior caused me concern. He always seemed to have lots of money, even though he only worked part-time for a lawn service. Plus he was always very guarded about his phone conversations and frequently excused himself. At first, I admired how seriously he took his lawn business, but then I began to have suspicions. Turns out they were valid concerns."

A wise woman is cautious in friendship (Proverbs 12:26). The word *cautious* used in this verse comes from a Hebrew word that means to seek out, search, or spy. As far as spying, I am all for doing background investigation. It's a prudent business practice. Employers and banks do it, why not us?

I'm not talking about asking for a resumé and doing a Social Security trace, but there are things you can do to probe and consider whether a romantic relationship is worthy of your heart's investment. You may feel like you're snooping, but you're not. Snooping is something you do when you have no reason other than sheer curiosity. You are investigating, so ask around about him. Notice who he hangs out with. Ask to meet his friends. Are his friends respectable or do they give you the creeps? By the way, you should especially be concerned if he doesn't have any friends.

Follow him on Facebook. Watch, observe, and watch some more. Most of your recon can be done in your conversations. Ask questions. Lots of questions. You are asking questions for a purpose, so they should be intentional. You're in an information-gathering mode for the purpose of evaluation. If his answers are vague and full of non-disclosure, stay away. Otherwise, store the information. Wait to see if his words agree with his actions. Don't be so gullible that you believe everything. And most importantly, put a guard on your heart until you and your advisors feel it's safe to proceed. Don't get emotionally involved until you have been able to scrutinize their character. You are a pearl of great price, bought with a price (see Matthew 13:45-46; 1 Corinthians 6:20). Don't throw your pearls to swine (Matthew 7:6)!

> **Don't get emotionally involved with any man until you have been able to scrutinize his character.**

The Five Fs

My friend Tom has a great strategy for evaluating potential love interests. He calls it the Five Fs. "I've dated too many girls whose faith was disingenuous," Tom explained. "There was some blood loss, but I'm still alive. Now, I have a system in place to protect myself from making the same mistakes again. When I meet a girl for lunch or dinner, I have my questions ready. It's straight up an interview without appearing like one."

When a girl gets Tom's interest, he begins the information-gathering procedure with a strategy. He intentionally asks her questions concerning the following five areas:

- ✦ Faith
- ✦ Family
- ✦ Friendships
- ✦ Finances
- ✦ Fitness

Tom explains the process:

When I ask a girl about her faith and she says, "Yeah, I go to church at New Hope," I'll casually ask, "Oh, really? Who's the pastor there?" If she stumbles around or can't answer right away, it may indicate she's not really serious about her faith.

As far as fitness goes, I'm trying to get an idea of her lifestyle choices. I'm not a gym rat, but I do a lot of kinetic activities, so I'll ask her questions to see if she's active. I'll also ask her what she likes to do for fun. I'm looking for similarities in the things we enjoy. My last girlfriend never played golf with me, even though I took dance lessons with her. She didn't take an interest in the things I enjoyed.

I also try to observe her in group settings. I can tell a lot about her by the kind of friends she has. If they're laid back, that's a good sign. If they're full of drama, though, she probably is too. Basically, the bottom line is if a girl is three for five Fs, I'm not wasting my time.

Tom's questions are prudent and deliberate. I applaud his screening process. He evaluates his date's character by asking her carefully considered and intentional questions. Like he said, it's basically an interview in a casual setting.

You can do the same thing and the guy doesn't have to know you are interviewing him. Even though you're the one asking all the questions, he'll get to do his favorite thing—talk about himself. He'll walk away thinking you're the interesting one, even though all you did was listen.

Try to ask as many open-ended questions as possible. Questions that only require a yes or no response don't facilitate dialogue. When he starts talking, listen. You're here to gather information, so resist the urge to interject too much. You're on an assignment. Listen and learn.

Questions about family, friends, and fitness (recreation and lifestyle) are the least intrusive and are good conversation starters, so you might want to start there. Don't force questions. If they don't seem to fit naturally into the conversation, save them for another time. The area of finance is more of an observation at first. Questions about money too soon in a relationship aren't appropriate, but there are other ways to gather information. Watch how he spends his money and take notice if he makes comments about being past due on things. If he pays child support, be attuned to his attitude when he talks about it. A responsible man won't have grievances about taking care of his obligations.

Questions that begin with, "Tell me about ..." are easy conversation openers. The person responding can tell you as little or as much as they want. If they like to talk, you'll learn a lot.

My son disagrees about asking too many questions, especially about faith. He thinks it's awkward. "I find it easier to make an intentional statement about my own faith and see if she takes the bait and continues the conversation," Garrett said. "For example, if she makes a comment about a conflict with a friend at work, I might say something like, 'Oh, I heard a great message at church about that.' It has to be legit, but I steer the conversation and see how they respond. People will talk about what's important to them. If she doesn't continue the conversation, she's probably not very grounded in her faith."

Maybe you're like Tom and want to ask questions. Or maybe you identify with Garrett, who wants to be more of an observer. Do whatever feels more comfortable to you. The main point is to keep an emotional distance and pay attention. Don't get emotionally involved with a man until you have sufficient time to evaluate whether or not his character is worthy.

THE DIFFERENCE BETWEEN CHARM AND CHARISMA

I can't warn women enough on this one. If you notice a man who has a special magnetism or presence, sirens ought to be going off in your head. When you feel the chemistry, watch out and slow down! Charm should be an alarm. Now, don't get me wrong—we all enjoy people who have charisma, but charm is much different.

> **Charm and chemistry are enticing qualities, but unless character is underneath that charm or chemistry, deceit will bite you like a snake.**

Charm and charisma both look the same on the surface, but charm has nothing underneath. Charm is superficial and deceptive (see Proverbs 31:30). Charm is Satan's counterfeit for charisma. Charisma is backed up with character and integrity. However, it's impossible to tell the difference without a deeper investigation.

There is no speed test to determine whether or not someone has character. The only way to tell is to hang around and evaluate their actions and reactions. Any man can behave well in a favorable climate, so we should put our emotions on hold until we determine that a man's character holds up under fire. In other words, how does he act when the pressure is on? When something doesn't go his way, is he easily angered or does he calmly adjust? When he makes a mistake, does he blame and accuse or does he take responsibility for his actions? When you say "no," does he respect your request? When you disagree with him, does he belittle and harass you?

Charm and chemistry are enticing qualities, but unless character is underneath that charm or chemistry, deceit will bite you like a snake. Chemistry is short term, but character provides longevity. Chemistry gets you the initial hook-up. Character ensures long-term relationship success. Sometimes chemistry is camouflaged. One person is needy and the other wants to rescue. That's not chemistry—that's codependency.

IS LOVE REALLY BLIND?

Marriage is the single most important contract and commitment we will ever make in life, apart from our salvation decision. Why, then, do so many of us enter without the consent and approval of those who know us best? Why do we risk the most important decision we will ever make to our own intellect?

Because love is blind.

At least according to Shakespeare.

Is Shakespeare's slogan grounded in truth, or is it merely a romantic notion endorsed to excuse a lack of discernment?

When it came to love, Samson was brainless, not blind. At least not in the beginning. He didn't get his eyes poked out until later in life. His first mistake was discounting the advice of his parents, but ultimately he failed in the marriage department because he was easily manipulated. Physically, Samson was the strongest man alive, and yet, in his soul he was weak and vulnerable. His first wife was a Philistine. Before the marriage was even consummated, he bribed his bride with a riddle in exchange for a new wardrobe, went on a killing spree, and then lost his wife to one of his groomsmen. Can't blame her. Sounds like Samson needed an anger management course.

Next he falls in love with Delilah. From day one, she begs him to disclose the secret of his strength. At first, Samson humors her with untruths. Judges 16:16 says, "She pressed him daily with her words and urged him, that his soul was vexed [annoyed] unto death" (KJV). Basically she nagged him until he finally gave in. Her pleas were so persistent that the incredible hulk was defeated by a woman's relentless rants.

Don't be like Samson who was so consumed with Delilah that he was deceived. There is a difference between real love and an unhealthy need to be loved. When we get caught up with an obsession to be loved, our vulnerability increases. The wrong relationship blinds us to reality and draws us away from God. Eventually, we develop an unhealthy soul tie that blinds us spiritually and compromises our destiny.

Delilah means feeble. Interesting … that's what Samson became. He lost his self-restraint; he let whatever guard he had over his heart completely evaporate. Consider James 1:14: "Every man is tempted when he is drawn away of his own lust and enticed" (KJV). Enticed comes from the Greek word *exelkō*, which means to draw out. It is used as a metaphor to describe how game is lured out of safety by hunters and fishermen. Likewise, men and women are lured from the safety of self-restraint by seductive words.

Words are hard to resist, especially in romance. We are most vulnerable when we are not surrounded by the safety that a wise counsel of friends provides. The old saying "Love is blind" really means that our discernment can be easily compromised in romantic relationships, but the way Shakespeare puts it makes it sound romantic. Being blindsided in romance is worse than a car wreck. Fortunately, there's insurance coverage. Proverbs calls it wisdom and understanding. I call it plain, old-fashioned accountability.

WISDOM AND UNDERSTANDING

"Wisdom and Understanding." Sounds like a great name for a legal firm. Unfortunately, as is usually the case with legal matters, in the realm of romance we generally don't look for counsel until we have issues. If we love our soul, however, we'll line up some advisors and keep them on retainer. That way, we'll always have good advice when we need it. There's nothing worse than being in a position where you desperately need advice and have no idea where to turn.

Proverbs 19:8 says, "He who gets wisdom loves his own soul; he who cherishes understanding prospers." The importance of counsel and accountability is key. When we isolate ourselves from godly counsel, our soul will not prosper. Isolation is the number-one enemy of soul-health. Where there is no counsel, the people fall (Proverbs 11:14). The way of a fool seems right to her, but a wise woman listens to counsel (Proverbs 12:15).

> *The wrong relationship blinds us to reality and draws us away from God.*

If you need legal advice, would you blindly pick an attorney out of the *Yellow Pages,* or would you ask around for referrals and check their case history? When paying for legal counsel, most of us carefully consider the expertise of the person we pay. We wouldn't pay a criminal defense attorney to give us advice in adoption proceedings. We choose our counsel based on their area of experience and expertise.

Of course, you would carefully select an expert to defend you. If you want to get physically fit, you hire a personal trainer with certification. If you want to get financially fit, you hire a certified financial planner. If you want to sell your house, you hire a realtor with a certification in real estate. If you want cosmetic surgery, you hire a specialist with certification in plastic surgery. Even if you want your nails done or a massage, the person you see must be certified. So let me ask you—if all of these things are important enough to require certification, are the people from whom you seek advice qualified to counsel you?

If you want to be wise, get counsel from the wise.

In matters regarding our soul-health, we need to carefully consider who we seek counsel from. Don't blindly accept advice from someone just because they go to your church or because they're your friend. First evaluate whether or not they have expertise in the area for which you need wisdom.

Are they wise, discreet, and moral? Do they have successful relationships? Are they respected, well-liked, and considerate? If they're overly critical and judgmental, beware. If they have low standards, their counsel will be full of compromise. If they have a string of broken relationships, go to someone else. You don't want the blind leading the blind. Like Tobias Smollett once said, "Some folks are wise and some are otherwise."

When seeking advice or counsel, it's our responsibility to call and ask for it. If we expect others to call and check up on us, we'll stay in isolation. Let me put it this way: If you're sick and need to see the doctor, you call and schedule an appointment. The doctor isn't going to call you. There are so many women who stay unhealthy emotionally because they won't make the effort to get soul-healthy.

–22–

Rehab for Rahab

"ACCOUNTABILITY BREEDS RESPONSE-ABILITY."
—STEPHEN R. COVEY

ACCOUNTABILITY IS A POPULAR TERM in church circles. Ask anyone if they agree with the concept of accountability and most will say, "Absolutely!" Ask Christians if they have an accountability partner, and many will give a resounding yes. But accountability is kind of like Botox...many want the look, but who really pays the price?

Accountability costs.

It costs us time, commitment, and comfort. It's not always easy to accept the advice of others, but it's important that we have wise counselors who will tell us the truth, even when it is not what we want to hear. Truth has the capacity to repel or compel. It either causes us to run away from God or run right to Him. The Word of God either brings opposition and resistance or conviction and repentance. This was certainly true in the case of the citizens of Jericho.

DOES TRUTH REPEL OR COMPEL YOU?

When the trumpet blasted in the battle of Jericho, the same sound of the trumpet that caused repentance and victory for God's people caused death and destruction for those in Jericho (see Joshua 6). How can the same message bring life to one and death to another? That is the nature of truth and the essence of God. His Word instills fear on those who disregard His voice. It causes us to hide our sin or expose it in repentance.

In Old Testament times, the trumpet was used to signify the presence of God. The Hebrew word for trumpet is *showphar*, which means to be pleasing or beautiful, to be bright or to glisten. It also means to scratch or scrape, to polish or incise. When we obey the mighty sound of God's voice, like the sound of a trumpet, His words will either resonate throughout our spirit or scratch our ears.

In the battle of Jericho, all who did not revere God were destroyed after the final trumpet blast caused the walls to come tumbling down. All except Rahab, the prostitute who hid the spies. She surrendered to the Lord and her entire household was spared.

Every friend she had was killed. Every remnant of her former life was shattered. Rahab lost everything. Only her life and the lives of her family members were spared. Instead of staying stuck in the past, however, Rahab chose to pick up the pieces of her life and move forward. She also chose to worship the God of Israel. Sometimes it takes losing everything to find life.

That's when Rahab started rehab.

Apparently, Rahab prospered. We don't hear anything else about her in the book of Joshua except that Joshua 6:25 tells us,

"She lives among the Israelites to this day." In the New Testament, however, Rahab is listed in the "Faith Hall of Fame" (Hebrews 11:31). Even though we don't have any details of Rahab's life, let's see if we can fill in the blanks a little. What kind of faith did it take for Rahab to leave her country, live among a people she didn't know and embrace their God? I don't think her faith was that large at first. It doesn't take much faith to do big things. Just a smidgen. Just mustard-seed size. If it took incredible faith to leave her country and follow the God of Israel, she wouldn't have stood a chance. She was a new convert, not a lifelong believer. She was a prostitute, a commoner, a sinner. Sinners don't start out with giant faith. They start out with surrender.

Rahab was like the rest of us. Over time, as she surrendered her beliefs, her fears, her pain and sorrow, her faith began to develop. Eventually, her faith stood the test of time and made a difference in generations to come.

Somewhere between the book of Joshua and the book of Hebrews, the faith of Rahab was so noteworthy, so remarkable and extraordinary, that she was permanently recorded. How did a prostitute develop that kind of extraordinary faith? I believe it was because Rahab was a woman who embraced the habit of accountability. She surrendered her own beliefs to a people who not only captured her, but captured her respect. To the people of Jericho, the Israelites were the enemy. But Rahab recognized something different—the power and favor of God evident in their life, something she desperately wanted.

After the walls of Jericho fell, Rahab immersed herself in the culture of believers. She absorbed their influence. She soaked up their faith. And little by little, the people she hung out with rubbed off on her. Who you hang out with will rub off on you. Who you hang with will influence your life. Rahab may not have understood the truth the Israelites embraced, but she recognized its power and made a decision to surrender to it. Often women search for counsel when a crisis makes them desperate, but as soon as their issues pass, they return to their former lifestyle. Rahab didn't do that. Her conversion was genuine.

> *Who you hang out with will rub off on you. Who you hang with will influence your life.*

She also lived among the people (Joshua 6:25). I don't believe this verse meant that she simply resided in the same city. Rahab wasn't just near believers. She was *with* believers. She enjoyed their fellowship and embraced their beliefs. Ultimately, living among the people influenced Rahab to follow the wisdom of their God. Take a look at who you hang out and fellowship with. The people around you influence and shape your life. Who you dwell with defines you. If they aren't building your faith or supporting your relationship with God, find some new friends.

YOU CAN BE A FAITH HALL OF FAMER

Obviously, there was something different about Rahab. Before her faith conversion, she was an innkeeper and a prostitute. Sounds like the gift of hospitality distorted by Satan. That's his specialty. He longs to know our calling as soon as we are born. The earlier the better. That way he can make plans to distort it.

He's not innovative enough to create something on his own. All he can do is twist God's design. Your life can be accounted for in the Faith Hall of Fame, too. Let's take a look at what it might that have looked like for Rahab.

I imagine Rahab as being a warm and affectionate woman. After she abandoned her previous lifestyle, she still loved being around people. Her gift of hospitality didn't evaporate after her conversion, but instead of influencing others with ungodly practices, she began sharing the love of God. She told the story of how she had heard about their miracle of deliverance—how the God of Israel helped His people cross the Red Sea on dry land escaping the pursuit of the Egyptians; how the spies came to her house; how she made an agreement with them for her family to be saved; and how God dramatically saved her life in the fall of Jericho.

Maybe she opened a coffee house for fellowship, giving herself and others opportunities to share their faith. A new convert usually spreads passion and fresh fire. In her later years, I can imagine her grandchildren gathered around her, sitting cross-legged on the floor, as she told them stories about the days of old and how the walls of Jericho fell. The Bible doesn't tell us how Rahab lived her life after the fall of Jericho, but one thing is certain: she influenced generations to come.

Speaking of being influenced by others, let's pause here for a moment and fast forward to Moab, a city on the other side of the Jordan River. Hang on with me for just a bit and you will see how the focus of your life can influence strangers, those you never meet, and even future generations.

THE TRUTH ABOUT RUTH

If you've ever felt neglected, abandoned, forgotten or alone, you'll appreciate Ruth's story. She grew up in a different time and place, but she felt the common fears we all face, particularly the fear of an uncertain future without a husband to provide for her. It doesn't matter if her story happened hundreds of years ago, we all bleed red.

Ruth grew up in Moab, a country despised by the Israelites. Moabites were enemies of Israel because they had not let the Israelites pass through their land during the exodus from Egypt. Ruth had a mother-in-law, Naomi, and a sister-in-law, Orpah. After an unfortunate string of deaths left all of them widowed, Naomi decided it was time to move.

As Naomi prepared to leave, Ruth began to panic. She couldn't bear to live without the hope she had seen evidenced in Naomi. Ruth had never heard such powerful stories of faith as those she had heard from Naomi, especially the one about the walls of Jericho falling down. She wanted to belong to a people like that. As Naomi turned to leave, Ruth blurted out in desperation, "Where you go I will go, and where you stay I will stay. Your people will be my people and your God my God" (Ruth 1:16).

Ruth was also a woman who embraced the habit of accountability. Despite the difficulties of leaving her old life behind, she persevered. The benefits of knowing God were worth the cost. The journey was long. It was unusual for two women to travel alone. When they finally arrived in Judah, they were the talk of the town.

"Is that Naomi? My goodness, we haven't seen her in years! And who is this with her?"

Word spread quickly. Text messaging will never be able to compete with the efficiency of a small town news network.

Ruth's reputation arrived the same day she did. Still, life was hard. Without a husband to provide for her, she was forced to glean the fields for food to eat. Picking up leftovers was the welfare system of the day. One day, she captured the interest of the owner of the field—Boaz, whom the Bible calls "a man of standing."

Boaz was captivated by Ruth.

"Why have you noticed me, a foreigner?" Ruth exclaimed.

"I've been told all about what you have done for your mother-in-law since the death of your husband—how you left your father and mother and your homeland and came to live with a people you did not know before. May the Lord repay you for what you have done" (Ruth 2:12).

Many were impressed with Ruth's character, but Boaz was deeply affected. In fact, he was so impressed with her that he was compelled to take care of her. What was it about Ruth that moved him?

I believe it's because ever since he was a young man, Boaz longed for a woman who embodied the character Ruth exhibited. His mother was like Ruth, and the thing he loved about the most influential woman in his life was the very thing he searched for in a wife.

Who was Boaz's mother? The book of Ruth doesn't tell us who she was. It only reveals that his father was Salmon (Ruth 4:21), but the New Testament gives us the answer in its genealogy report beginning with the Gospel of Matthew. Matthew's obsession with ancestry opens with a report detailing forty-two generations of who begat whom, something I used to skip over entirely to get to the interesting stuff. But there was one day I noticed a lineage shocker tucked in between Salmon and Boaz. Suddenly I was forever grateful Matthew was an obsessive-compulsive historian. He reveals a secret in verse five that gives us insight into why Boaz was so captivated by Ruth—Boaz's mother was a woman who had done the same thing Ruth had done. His mother had left her homeland to come live with a people she did not know before. His mother had left the gods of her country to worship the God of Israel.

His mother was Rahab.

I can imagine that as a young boy Boaz often sat on his mother's lap and listened over and over again to the story of how she had left everything behind to follow the God of Israel. How he had prayed for a woman like that. And now, the character he cherished most about his mother—her faith and commitment to accountability—was evident in a foreigner.

Ruth was interested in Boaz as well and sought Naomi's advice. "Here's what you need to do," began Naomi. "Take a bath and put on some of your best perfume. Then pick out your favorite outfit and go to the field tonight. Boaz is going to be there."

There you have it, ladies. Permission in the Word of God to look good and smell good for our men! Some courting strategies are timeless.

But some romantic gestures make no sense at all today—like Naomi's next instructions.

"Wait until he is done eating and drinking and go lie down by his feet."

I'm sure Naomi knew how to catch a man in her day, but I'm also quite confident that that advice wouldn't cut it today. Times have definitely changed. A century ago, she may have said, "Drop your hankie, honey." Today, her advice may have been to send a cyber-wink. But you get the point. Naomi was urging Ruth to make her presence known.

Later than night, Boaz noticed someone at his feet.

"His heart leapt with excitement. She wanted *him*. She hadn't gone after the younger man who had the first right to redeem her property and accept her as his wife. The next morning, Boaz rushed to the city gate to make his intentions known. Before he could marry Ruth, the other man had to deny his right. When the man arrived, Boaz quickly gathered the elders of the town to witness his offer. "Naomi is selling the piece of land that belonged to our brother Elimelech," Boaz began. "You have the first right to purchase the property, but since I am next in line, please let me know your intentions."

He could only hope that the man wasn't aware that Ruth and Naomi came as a set. She and her mom were a package deal. "Just to make sure you understand," he continued, "on the day you buy the land, you also acquire the dead man's widow."

This scene so reminds me of *Let's Make a Deal*. I can just picture game show host Monty Hall explaining that everything that comes behind door number two is now yours.

"Oh, well. I wasn't aware. Unfortunately," the other man replied, "redeeming Ruth's property will jeopardize my estate. I'm afraid I'll have to pass."

Apparently the additional asset was a deal breaker.

Boaz was free to take Ruth as his wife. A broad smile spread across his face as he handed over his sandal to legalize his transaction—another crazy tradition common back in that day.

Soon, Boaz and Ruth were married and Ruth gave birth to a son. They named him Obed. He was the father of Jesse, the father of David. Generations later, the Messiah was born.

It all began with the faith of a prostitute.

THE IMPACT OF ONE LIFE

Do you think Rahab ever thought about the impact her life would make? After all, she was but a prostitute, a reject. Who could she influence? Certainly, no one would have ever predicted that the Messiah would come from her lineage. But Rahab was willing to leave behind the wisdom of her culture. She was willing to forsake her lifestyle and the gods her society worshipped. She was willing to leave everything behind to follow the God of Israel and listen to the counsel of the wise.

What about Ruth? Do you think she ever thought about the impact her life would make? After all, she was a Moabite, a foreigner, an enemy of God's people. Who could she influence? Certainly, no one would have ever predicted that the Messiah would come from her lineage. But Ruth was willing to leave behind the wisdom of her culture. She was willing to forsake her lifestyle and the gods her society worshipped. She was willing to leave everything behind to follow the God of Israel and listen to the counsel of the wise.

What about you? Have you ever thought about the impact your decision to embrace the habit of accountability would have on this culture and even future generations? We must never doubt the impact we can make when we choose to acknowledge God's favor, surrender to His will, and live among His people. Our life can leave a legacy for generations to come. We can influence people we will never meet.

Rahab and Ruth were two women who embraced the habit of accountability and made a tremendous impact—women who chose to surrender their trust to the faith and wisdom of others. Little did they know what a difference their surrender would make on generations to come. I can't wait to meet them in heaven and let them know how many times I've told their story to women like you. Do you see the value of accountability? Your love story can make a difference too. Will you surrender it to wisdom?

-23-

Strengthening Accountability

PRACTICING THE HABIT of accountability allows you to protect your will by surrendering your choices to wise counsel. Exercising accountability is like purchasing an insurance policy for your heart. You have coverage when a storm threatens to destroy your soul. You'll never be so wise that you don't need the wisdom of others. Check out what the Scriptures say about this soul-healthy habit and then use the action points to protect your most valuable asset—your heart.

ACCOUNTABILITY SCRIPTURE TRUTHS

+ "Though one may be overpowered, two can defend themselves. A cord of three strands in not quickly broken" (Ecclesiastes 4:12).

+ "Where no counsel [is], the people fall: but in the multitude of counselors [there is] safety" (Proverbs 11:14 KJV).

✦ "Plans fail for lack of counsel, but with many advisers they succeed" (Proverbs 15:22).

✦ "Wounds from a friend can be trusted, but an enemy multiplies kisses" (Proverbs 27:6).

✦ "Blessed is the man who does not walk in the counsel of the wicked or stand in the way of sinners or sit in the seat of mockers. He is like a tree planted by streams of water, which yields its fruit in season and whose leaf does not wither. Whatever he does prospers" (Psalm 1:1, 3).

✦ "The way of a fool seems right to him, but a wise man listens to advice" (Proverbs 12:15).

✦ "As iron sharpens iron, so one man sharpens another" (Proverbs 27:17).

✦ "He who gets wisdom loves his own soul; he who cherishes understanding prospers" (Proverbs 19:8).

✦ "Listen to advice and accept instruction, and in the end you will be wise" (Proverbs 19:20).

ACCOUNTABILITY ACTION POINTS

Remember, accountability is the practice of protecting your will by surrendering your choices to wise counsel. If you have trouble with the habit of accountability, try the following action points to strengthen your submission to godly wisdom.

Pray for a Mentor

Ask the Lord to direct you to a trustworthy person of the same sex who will challenge you in your walk with the Lord. Ask that person to be your accountability partner. Establish a suitable schedule of contact and take the initiative to contact her on a regular basis.

Establish Godly Friendships

A network of firm believers allows you to obtain godly counsel when you need encouragement, advice, or prayer. Don't isolate yourself. Lonely people are prey for the enemy's schemes. If you don't have enough friends, get involved. Join a small group, a Bible study, or become a volunteer.

Nurture Established Relationships

Is there a relationship you've put on the back burner? Take time to nurture those that are important to you. Friendship is like a book: it takes a few seconds to burn, but years to write.

Give Others Permission to Put You on the SPOT

Give trustworthy friends and people you respect permission to put you on the spot. Ask them to speak into your life and confront you when they see you making unwise decisions. Consider easing any potential awkwardness by giving them a preset list of questions you want them to ask you, especially concerning areas in which you struggle. For example, if you struggle with sexual temptation, give them permission to ask if you are practicing sexual restraint. If you struggle with addiction issues, have them ask about your sobriety.

If you prefer, have them ask you the following four questions using the SPOT acronym:

S   Are you **serving** the Lord?

P   Are you **praying** daily?

O   Are you **obeying** the Word?

T   Are you **training** for the goal?

Have a Forewarn System

Establish a policy with your mentor about how you will handle sexually tempting situations. Advise your accountability partner of any dates you have and call the next day to let her know how it went. When we know we're accountable to someone, our motivation to maintain purity is stronger.

Take Inventory

Take a regular personal inventory of your own life by examining your behavior. Look over the following list and confess any evidence of blame, bitterness, selfishness, jealousy, idolatry, gossip, pride, addictive behavior, sexual immorality, seductive behavior or dress, strife, hatred, anger, or rage. Pray about your issues and ask the Lord to give you insight and wisdom so you don't repeat the same mistakes.

Pinpoint False Beliefs

Take note of areas where the Word of God is not your standard. In order to get victory in that area, you must find the root of your false belief. Until you do, the enemy can hold you captive to sin. Once you identify the false belief, begin to erase it by meditating on Scripture and replacing it with truth.

Set Goals for Your Future

Identify weaknesses you want to improve. Set realistic goals to accomplish them. Write them down and review them with your accountability partner monthly. Without a focus and a vision for your future, it's hard to recognize detours and you won't easily notice when you've veered off the path. Don't wait for a hardship and then try to figure out what to do. Make accommodations for things that could go wrong and plan ahead how you will respond.

QUESTIONS TO PONDER

1. What blind spots have you noticed in your own romantic relationships?

2. What are some of your weaknesses that hinder your judgment of character?
    a. Rushing into a relationship too soon.
    b. Being overly trusting.
    c. Misguided compassion.
    d. Ignoring the advice of family and friends.
    e. Haven't quite figured it out yet, but I keep making the same mistakes over and over again.

3. What are some things you can do to be cautious in friendship and guard you heart?

4. Which of the Five Fs (faith, family, friendships, finances, fitness) is most important to you? Why? Which is the least? Why?

5. What do you think about the common expression that love is blind? Do you think you can control who you fall in love with?

6. It's been said that we will be the same person in five years except for the people we meet and the books we read. If that's true, what people do you want to sprinkle in your life?

As a soul-healthy woman you embrace the habit of accountability. You know that true wisdom comes from the combination of God's wisdom flowing through both the Holy Spirit and the counsel of others. You aren't afraid or too proud to acknowledge that you have areas of vulnerability and want to cover your weaknesses with the oversight of others who will look out for your best interests. Accountability then positions you to receive the most powerful guidance of all—the direction of God for your life.

—24—

STEP NUMBER 7:
Yes

YES: THE PRACTICE OF SURRENDERING MY WILL
AND ALLOWING GOD TO LEAD MY LIFE.

DISCERNING AND SAYING YES to God's direction for my life has not always been easy. When I'd have my quiet time and situate myself to hear His voice, half of my dialogues with the Lord would end in debate with my three best friends—Me, Myself, and I. *Was that really God talking or just Me, Myself, and I on three-way? Do I go this way or that way? Which is it, Lord? Is that You or the voice of the enemy or the voice of my own selfish reasoning?*

Truth be known, for years I was afraid of God's direction. I just knew He was going to call me to Africa or the convent, so I had my own agenda, my own map plotting out my destiny. It was years before I realized that saying yes to God's direction for my life was better than anything I could ask, think, or imagine (Ephesians 3:20). He loves me and has a customized journey and destiny for my life. And He does for you too.

As far as relationships were concerned, it never occurred to me to ask God His opinion about who I dated. If I had, I would have avoided much heartache. Thankfully, I've learned how to discard my own plans, especially in regard to relationships, and say yes to His direction. You can too. It's not difficult. We just have to pay attention to His navigational commands. He steers our lives in many ways. Sometimes it's through the Bible, through a sermon, or through a song. Sometimes it's a dream or vision. Other times, He speaks through nature, other people, or even painful situations. Sometimes, even when it goes against our own logic and desire, He asks us to sit still for a while.

Alicia knows this full well. As an Auburn University college student, Alicia couldn't help but notice that most students dated frequently, but she had clear instructions from the Lord. She was to wait on God because He was preparing her for her husband.

"It was hard to see so many couples out on the weekends, so one year, my Christian girlfriends and I made a pact," she said. "Valentine's Day was coming up, and we all promised each other we would go on a date with the Lord. When we got back we would share what He said to us. It was such an awesome experience that it became my Valentine's Day tradition all through college and into the year after I graduated."

In 1997, Alicia had just started working for Kodak as an engineer. "Even though I was in Rochester, New York, I got all dressed up and took my journal to dinner with me," she continued. "That's when the Lord spoke to me and said, 'I'm pleased with your purity in mind and devotion to me. I am now releasing you to be married.' I couldn't believe what I had just written. At first I laughed because there was absolutely no one on my radar. I felt like Sarai when the angel of the Lord said she would have a baby in the next year.

"The Lord told me to commit these things to faithful ears and that my own faith would be released as I proclaimed it to others. So I did. I called my friends and told them, 'This is strange, but by this time next year, I feel like I'll no longer be single.'"

Alicia had met a man named Clarence years earlier in Atlanta, Georgia, at an Impact conference sponsored by Campus Crusade for Christ. He attended school at Southern Nazarene University in Bethany, Oklahoma, and the two had exchanged emails over the previous couple of years, but it was all casual—nothing romantic.

Then things changed.

"We hadn't talked on the phone, so when Clarence called the next month and wanted to see me, I knew he must be the one," she said. "Sure enough, he proposed a few months later, and we were married on July 4, 1998."

Today, Clarence and Alicia have been married for sixteen years. They have three children and lead a thriving marriage ministry. "I often wondered what would have happened if I hadn't waited on the Lord," said Alicia. "It was hard to surrender my will and say yes to His direction for my life, but Clarence was definitely worth the wait. I know through the difficulties I've experienced, I can encourage other women that God's promises are worth the wait."

Listen to the Prompts

The habit of yes is the habit of surrendering our will to God and allowing Him to lead our lives.

The best way to follow God's lead is to learn to recognize the prompts, the inner witness and leading of the Holy Spirit. This doesn't mean we should rush out and follow the prompts in haste. We need to be certain it's actually God speaking to us.

In his book *Experiencing God*, Henry Blackaby says, "God speaks to us through the Holy Spirit. He uses the Bible, prayer, circumstances, and the church (other believers). No one of these methods of God's speaking is, by itself, a clear indicator of God's directions. But when God says the same thing through each of these ways, you can have confidence to proceed."[22] What Blackaby is saying is that having confidence we've heard God's voice is essential. Multiple divine indicators give us humans the heavenly assurance we need.

> *Multiple divine indicators give us humans the heavenly assurance we need.*

When the Lord knit my heart together with John, the Holy Spirit gave me an inner knowing that I was going to marry him well before he proposed. But it wasn't just my own knowing that gave me that confidence. Our friends and family all saw the obvious connection, and one time a lady at church we had never met made a beeline to meet us after service. She introduced herself and said, "I just had to come meet you both. There was a light shining around you." God also confirmed His will for our relationship in other unique ways. On several occasions, John and I would discover that God had given each of us the same Scripture or word of encouragement. It was this synchronization of our spiritual life that made it hard to deny that God was endorsing our relationship.

It's hard to contest that God is directing your life when everywhere you turn you're hearing and seeing the same thing. Isaiah 30:21 says, "Whether you turn to the right or to the left, your ears will hear a voice behind you, saying, 'This is the way; walk in it.'" The use of the word *ears* in this verse comes from a Hebrew word that doesn't just mean your physical ears. It also means "the receiver of divine revelation." In other words, hearing from God doesn't always mean you will hear an audible voice. It's usually more of an inner witness, an understanding or a perception.

The first time you sense a new directive from God, put your ears on high alert. First, you'll want to rule out the voice of the tumultuous triplets— me, myself and I. Then, listen for further evidence of His direction.

Wait for Confirmation

Sometimes, despite obvious signs, we need more evidence that God really is directing us. Is it wrong to want proof that God is speaking? Or is wanting a confirmation merely a modern-day version of doubt? Let's examine what the Bible says about confirmations.

If a confirmation is an endorsement, authentication, or supporting evidence, I see it used all throughout Scripture. Even though the word *confirmation* only appears twice in the King James Version and not at all in the New International Version, God displays signs and wonders to prove His point.

For example, in Scripture when the Holy Spirit wants to reveal Himself, He provides many convincing proofs. In the first chapter of the Gospel of Luke, the angel of the Lord visited Mary to announce her divine conception. He also gave her information she otherwise couldn't have known to verify His prediction (as if seeing an angel wasn't proof enough). He told her that her barren cousin, Elizabeth, was six months pregnant. After Mary ran to

Elizabeth's house, Elizabeth was filled with the Holy Ghost as soon as she heard Mary's voice. Then the angel visited Joseph to confirm the divine conception so Joseph wouldn't proceed with his intentions to quietly divorce Mary.

In the Old Testament, Gideon tested the directive issued by the angel (Judges 6:39). He wasn't used to hearing from God and needed to know *for sure* the angel was really from God. He told God he was going to put a wool fleece outside his tent. He asked God to make the wool wet with the morning dew but leave everything else dry. God indulged Gideon's doubt. Then Gideon begged for one more test. This time he wanted God to make the fleece dry and the ground covered with dew. Perhaps Gideon went to the extreme, but God obliged.

When Abraham sent his servant to go find a wife for his son, Isaac, the servant prayed and asked God for a sign. "When I ask for a drink at the spring, let your chosen one be the one who offers water for my camels as well." This wasn't a haphazard request. The servant was searching for a woman of character, a woman with a heart to serve. When the servant met Rebekah at the well and she offered to water his camels, he knew she was the Lord's chosen. The match was obvious to Rebekah's family as well. "This is from the Lord," they agreed (see Genesis 24:50).

When God wants us to believe, He sends many convincing proofs; however, I don't believe we always get to order the type of sign we want (see Matthew 16:4). Even though it worked for Abraham's servant, it's faith that builds our walk with Christ. If we pay closer attention to the promptings of the Holy Spirit, we will be able to discern His lead. And like a dance, the closer we are to our partner, the easier it is to feel His lead.

Sometimes we have to test the waters. Peter did. When he saw Jesus walking on the water, at first he thought Jesus was a ghost. "Lord, if it's you, tell me to come to you" (Matthew 14:28). Sometimes we doubt. Sometimes we don't hear the first time He calls. One of the greatest prophets in the Old Testament, Samuel, missed the voice of God the first three times He spoke (1 Samuel 3:8). Sometimes we completely miss it, but that's all part of the process. God always allows retakes. No matter how many times we fail, He always gives us another chance.

Press Past Frustrations

John was married twice before we met. His failed marriages made him feel like a two-time loser, so he worked hard to overcome the shame through counseling and inner healing. Despite his best efforts to improve his soul-health, however, he still brought a bit of baggage into our relationship. It remained neatly packed away until we had our first marital "disagreement"—a major blowout over a minor issue. On this particular day, I was supposed to pick him up after work because we had just sold his car, but he was so angry he refused to let me. Even though John knew God brought us together, the familiar "grab-your-bags-and-run" mentality was hardwired to his ideology. Instead, John insisted on renting a car. He walked over five miles in 104-degree weather to collect his thoughts—and avoid me.

> *No matter how many times we fail, He always gives us another chance.*

"My fury and confused convictions made me want to run more than ever," said John. "Despite the fact that it was a blistering hot day, it was chilly compared to my anger and insecurities. I had always worried so much about what people thought about me. I wanted everyone to think I had it all together, but inside I still felt like a mess. In the past, when conflicts in my relationships threatened to expose my insecurities, I slammed my suitcase shut."

As I watched an airplane take off from the nearby airport and thought about all the baggage onboard, I heard the Lord say, "Are you always going to be this way?"

That certainly got John's attention. "I knew what He was talking about. I had been on this flight before. Twice. I already knew where it led and, the truth was, I didn't want to be in the same place again. I had always been a runner—running away from conflict to find my place of safety. I thought it was easier to start over than to press past the pain.

"With rivers of sweat running down my forehead, shoulders, and back, I realized if I chose to keep my baggage, I'd never be able to move forward. I couldn't grow if I didn't face the pain. I surrendered my baggage that day and decided to trust the Pilot to get me to my destination."

John describes the changes he's undergone this way: "Today I don't care if others know I'm not perfect. God's opinion of me is the only one that matters. It's such a relief to finally be free from the weight of my baggage and the concern of maintaining 'my image.' God now uses my open suitcase to challenge others not to run away from their problems. Don't run. Say yes to your pain. There's freedom in surrender."

Just because God puts two people together doesn't mean there won't be difficulties. Often love junkies want to bail at the first sign of trouble. They may think, *This can't be God's will if we are going through this.* Many relationships end outside of God's will because one or both partners aren't willing to press past frustrations. It's not always easy, but dealing with conflicts can make us and our relationship stronger. Conflicts are just the manifestation of a problem that needs to be addressed. It's God's way of purifying us. If we ignore it, deny it or push it back down, like a jack-in-the-box, it will pop up its head again later. It's best to acknowledge it and surrender it to God.

John dealt with a lot of generational shame. He learned it from his parents. They were highly critical and ashamed of his divorces. John felt terrible that he'd been such a disappointment to them. Ironically, he didn't find out until after they both passed away that they each had been married previously. They had never unpacked their own suitcases.

Finding out that they hid their shame about their divorces for over fifty years made John even more determined not to succumb to the habits he learned from them. The next time disagreements in our marriage tempted him to run, John recognized God was giving him another opportunity to release bad habits. Instead stuffing the shame, he confessed his fault and received God's grace to change. Likewise, when God allows issues in your life to surface, refuse the shame. God uses the heat of adversity to expose the junk in our trunk and purify us, so don't stuff your issues back down. Surrender them to Him and refuse failure.

Refuse Failure

Kara was in a verbally abusive marriage for twenty-one years. "Hope was not a part of my life," she recalled. "I felt like such a failure. For years I lived in a pit of depression, and then . . . my life took a turn for the worse."

Kara was diagnosed with breast cancer. In one month she lost her breasts, her hair, and her career. "I didn't even feel like living," said Kara, "but after attending a support group at the hospital, God put it in my heart to start a faith-based support group at my church for cancer survivors as well as for caregivers."

Kara led the group for ten years. "I don't know what I would have done without the support they provided. God used them to pull me out of the pit of despair. Through thirteen surgeries, two Mayo Clinic trips, and a battle with Transverse Myelitis that landed me in a wheelchair, I can now walk, run, and even wear heels! Today, I see lots of things differently. When I look at my ex-husband, I realize he is the one with cancer. His soul is terminally ill. That's why he was so manipulative and verbally abusive. It wasn't because I was inadequate. It's because hurting people hurt people. Jeremiah 29:11 has become my life verse. Now when I look at myself in the mirror, I see a future instead of a failure."

Like John and Kara, if you're going to surrender your life to God or say yes to His direction, you have to be willing to press through the pain. Unfortunately, there are no shortcuts, U-turns, or scenic turnouts, but pain has a purpose in redirecting your destiny. Forget the past, press on, and look forward to what lies ahead. Reach the end of your race and receive the heavenly prize for which God is calling you (Philippians 3:13-14).

Say Yes to God's Direction for Your Life

Despite all the relationship issues I've endured in my own life, today I'm thankful for every tear I've cried and every trial I've endured. When I think back to the day in 1988 when my first husband confronted me about my unfaithfulness, I had no idea that the pain would produce such purpose. Who would have ever thought a relationship addict would teach the next generation how to be soul-healthy? Ironically, it's God's specialty to pick the least likely to succeed. If He can use a murderer of Christians to write half of the New Testament, list a prostitute in the Hebrew Hall of Fame, and use a woman at the well to cause many to believe in the Messiah, He can use you, too! No matter how many failed relationships you've had, no matter how far you've run from God, no matter how many times you've messed up—He can turn it all around.

I'm tremendously inspired by the apostle Paul. He endured more adversity than most can imagine, but in the final analysis he writes in Philippians 1:19, "I will continue to rejoice, for I know . . . what has happened to me will turn out for my deliverance." God's promise is the same for all of His children, and you are no exception. What has happened in your life, God is able to use to liberate your soul.

My heartaches have produced perseverance. My trials have made me stronger. Today, I'm an overcomer. And without reservation, I can say I'd do it all over again to be who I am in Christ today. I, like Paul, truly believe that though not pleasant at the time, everything I've endured has turned out for my deliverance. I believe the same for you. No matter what you are facing, God is able to make whatever has happened to you turn out for your deliverance. Say yes to God. Continue to rejoice and don't turn back. He has amazing plans for you.

–25–

Strengthening
Your Yes

YOU ARE ABOUT TO EMBRACE the final step to breaking the toxic love cycle. By surrendering your will and allowing God to lead your life, your life will dramatically change for the better. I'm praying for you, sister. I believe God can reveal Himself to you in such a powerful way that you'll never be the same again.

YES SCRIPTURE TRUTHS

+ "Trust in the LORD with all your heart and lean not on your own understanding; in all your ways acknowledge him, and he will make your paths straight. Do not be wise in your own eyes; fear the LORD and shun evil. This will bring health to your body and nourishment to your bones" (Proverbs 3:5-8).

+ "The heart of the discerning acquires knowledge; the ears of the wise seek it out" (Proverbs 18:15).

✦ " 'For I know the plans I have for you'," declares the LORD, " 'plans to prosper you and not to harm you, plans to give you hope and a future' " (Jeremiah 29:11).

✦ "In his heart a man plans his course, but the LORD determines his steps" (Proverbs 16:9).

✦ "For to me, to live is Christ and to die is gain" (Philippians 1:21).

✦ "Therefore, my brothers, be all the more eager to make your calling and election sure. For if you do these things, you will never fall" (2 Peter 1:10).

✦ "For God's gifts and his call are irrevocable" (Romans 11:29).

✦ "Being confident of this, that he who began a good work in you will carry it on to completion until the day of Christ Jesus" (Philippians 1:6).

✦ "Consider it pure joy, my brothers, whenever you face trials of many kinds, because you know that the testing of your faith develops perseverance. Perseverance must finish its work so that you may be mature and complete, not lacking anything" (James 1:2-4).

✦ "We must pay more careful attention, therefore, to what we have heard, so that we do not drift away. God also testified to it by signs, wonders and various miracles, and by gifts of the Holy Spirit distributed according to his will" (Hebrews 2:1, 4).

YES ACTION POINTS

Remember, the habit of yes is the practice of surrendering our will and allowing God to guide our lives. If you have trouble with the habit of yes, try the following action points to strengthen your willingness to surrender.

Create an Atmosphere

Practice being in God's presence. Do this by creating an atmosphere of praise and prayer. Then with a quiet heart, wait for Him to speak. Just as your relationship with your friends grows as you spend time with them, your intimacy with God will grow the more time you spend with Him.

Make a Gratitude List

Often fear and uncertainty make us hesitant about surrendering to God's direction. Think about the things God has done for you in the past. Write them down and reflect on them frequently. Whenever doubts arise, take out your list again. Watch your faith to surrender to His direction increase as you meditate on His faithfulness.

Practice Surrender

If you are having difficulty with surrender, ask the Lord to show you something you can surrender that is just beyond the measure of faith you currently have. Developing a lifestyle of surrender takes faith and practice. You won't be able to surrender something significant if you've never surrendered something small. As you practice a lifestyle of surrender, however, soon you'll be able to surrender things you never dreamed possible.

"Surrender is like learning to read," says Jeannie, a fifth-grade teacher. "I especially have to stretch my students who are reading below grade level. I don't allow those who read at the fourth-grade level to read third-grade level books. The only way to improve their reading level is for them to select something just above their current reading level. That way they stay challenged."

What could you surrender today?

Do a Trial Run

If you are uncertain what God's purpose or will is for your life, do a trial run. Test serving in various areas and pay attention to how fulfilling each activity is for you. We all have different gifts according to the grace given us (Romans 12:6). You'll feel joy and godly contentment when you are functioning where God wants you. His grace and empowerment accompanies His will for your life and compliments your unique set of talents and life experiences.

Find Encouragement

Sometimes we feel like we are the only one dealing with relationship issues or challenges. Pursue acquaintances with others who you know have overcome the issue you struggle with. Join a small group that addresses how to conquer the concerns you face. Encourage yourself in the Lord by reading books or biographies of other Christians with whom you identify. Knowing others have traveled similar paths proves we are not alone.

Pay Attention to Perceived Direction

Keep a journal of how you perceive God to be directing you in your relationships. Jot down anytime you think He is giving you additional insight. Over time, you may recognize repeated directions, advice, and signs that confirm His will.

Talk it Over

Discuss what you perceive as God's direction for your relationship issues with a trusted advisor, accountability partner, or friend. Often the wisdom and insight that other people bring gives us fresh perspective and clarity.

Pray for Vision

Ask God to give you a vision for your future. Pray that He will confirm it in such a way that your hope and confidence is anchored.

QUESTIONS TO PONDER

1. When you are veering off of God's path for your life, how quickly do you discern His redirect?

    a. His voice is like the voice on my GPS. As soon as I've made a wrong turn, I hear Him announce, "Rerouting, rerouting."

    b. I usually don't notice until I'm miles off course.

    c. I'm typically so focused on the scenery, I never hear a word.

2. Do you have a life verse, a Scripture that profoundly speaks to your heart about God's plan and direction for your life? What is it and why is it so significant to you? If you don't have a life verse, what are some of your favorite Scriptures?

3. What areas of your soul-health are the most healthy? Which need the most improvement?
   a. Identity
   b. Forgiveness
   c. Imagination
   d. Prayer
   e. Resolve
   f. Accountability
   g. Yes

4. Through reading this book, how has your awareness about your own soul-health changed?

5. Have you ever experienced generational shame like John did? How did it affect your life? Have you been able to release it? If so, how?

6. What are some of the things in the area of relationships you have surrendered to Christ? Has it been difficult or easy? How was your faith challenged?

7. Has God recently asked you to surrender anything? What was your response?

8. Have you endured any relationship issues that, although painful at the time, you can now see how God used them for your deliverance? If you feel comfortable sharing, describe how God brought you through.

Even when God's direction for a soul-healthy woman's life seems to go in the opposite direction of where her flesh wants to go, she is willing to release her desires because she understands that God's ways are higher than her ways. Saying yes to God's direction doesn't mean she's perfect. In fact, she chooses to follow God's vision because she realizes how imperfect and incompetent she is. In her own wisdom, she's made so many mistakes she's come to believe that it's far better to rely on God and put her trust in His will for her life. And ultimately, she's realized a powerful conclusion: When a love junkie surrenders her will, she finally gets what she's always wanted—the freedom to be a confident, soul-healthy woman.

-26-

Ditch the Drama

I REMEMBER THE FIRST TIME I went to a full-service salon and paid to get my hair highlighted. I was certain I had finally arrived. I looked like a million bucks when I stepped out of the salon, but the next day when I woke up and looked in the mirror, I experienced sheer horror. After tossing and turning all night, my hair looked nothing like it had the day before when the professional styled it. It was a mess. That's when I headed for the shower to shampoo, rinse, and repeat.

So it is with our soul-health. No matter how much progress we make, there will be times when we have to deal with a mess. That's when we take our issue and follow the instructions in this book—undo, review, and repeat.

Maintaining our soul-health takes work. Today my blonde has turned gray and requires even more upkeep, but I'm not shaving my head just because I don't like the color. I may have to spend a bit more time to get the desired results, but here's my point. Strive for excellence instead of expecting perfection. Excellence is doable, but perfection will drive you crazy. In reality, the only place people (or hairstyles for that matter) look perfect is in the movies.

I'd also like to encourage you to keep this book as a resource. The steps to breaking the toxic love cycle are easy to remember since they spell "If-I-Pray": identity, forgiveness, imagination, prayer, resolve, accountability, and yes. When struggles threaten the return of old habits, review the steps in your mind and try to pinpoint which of the habits your issue is trying to compromise. Then flip to that chapter and review the Scriptures and action points to work through your issue.

When you continue to apply the seven steps to breaking the toxic love cycle, you'll see a shift happen in your soul-health. Your confidence increases as your source of identity shifts. You care more about what Christ thinks about you than what others do. You no longer need a relationship or marriage to provide assurance. You may *want* a relationship, but when it's no longer a necessity you won't be tempted to compromise.

> *Unlike the love junkie, the soul-healthy no longer needs a relationship or marriage to provide self-assurance and self-worth.*

You learn to forgive quickly instead of hanging on to bitterness. You'd rather have the peace that forgiveness brings than the sting of bitterness. You imagine yourself and your circumstances through God's perspective, rather than allowing vain imaginations to thrust you into despair. You pray more. You ask for revelation to empower your resolve and you're not afraid to submit to accountability. You see the red flags to which you were previously oblivious. If you're single, you won't pick a man in desperation just because he's moving and breathing; you'll be able to move and breathe because you've picked a soul-healthy man. If you're married, conflicts in your marriage don't equate to failure. You don't obsess over issues because they no longer define you.

And finally, you're more patient because you've learned to say yes to God's direction. Ultimately, as a soul-healthy woman, you're no longer dependent on a relationship for contentment. Once and for all, you've learned how to ditch the drama and find the love you've always wanted.

WHAT ABOUT MY SCARS?

One year, John and I bought Garrett a scooter for Christmas. The scooter was basically a motorized skateboard with a steering wheel—an accident waiting to happen. And it did. One of our neighbors brought Garrett home one afternoon with a big gash over his eye. I freaked out. Garrett grinned. Behind the blood, mud, and dried tears smeared all over his forehead, he almost seemed a bit proud. Later that week, one of John's body-builder friends came by the house.

"What happened to your eye, dude?" Mark asked.

"Had an accident on my scooter," said Garrett as he nonchalantly stood up a little taller. "Spun out in some gravel."

Mark rolled up his sleeve revealing a scar on his arm. "This happened to me when I was about your age."

"I got another one on my knee," said Garrett as he quickly bent down to roll up his jean leg. "It's from a car wreck I was in when I was five."

I listened as Garrett and Mark traded scar stories and realized they had a completely different perspective about the pain they'd endured. These wounded warriors bragged about their scars. To them, their scars were medals of honor, and they wore them proudly like tattooed trophies. They didn't remember the pain. They remembered the victory.

I snapped a picture of the dangerous duo so I'd never forget what I learned that day. Sure, the mistakes and hurts in my life have left many scars. But now I see them differently. Thanks to Garrett and Mark, my perspective has changed. My scars aren't painful reminders of my past. They are evidence I have survived, proof I've prevailed.

The other day I told John it would be neat if we could come up with an acronym for the word *scar*. In ten seconds flat, he blurted out, "A scar is a Second Chance At Restoration." Indeed scars are about restoration. Let the healing begin.

Notes

1. Wes Hopper, "Repeating Patterns in Relationships," www.you-can-have-it.com/blog/repeating-patterns-in-relationships.

2. Lisa Bevere, *Kissed the Girls and Made Them Cry* (Nashville: Thomas Nelson, 2002), 86.

3. Bill Urell, "12 Signs and Symptoms of an Addictive Relationship," http://addictionrecoverybasics. com/12-signs-and-symptoms-of-an-addictive-relationship.

4. Lisa Bevere, *Kissed the Girls and Made Them Cry*, 90.

5. Shannon Ethridge, *Every Woman's Battle* (Colorado Springs: WaterBrook, 2003), 35.

6. Neil Clark Warren, *Finding the Love of Your Life* (New York: Pocket Books, 1992), 3.

7. John D. Moore, "The Obsessive Love Wheel," http:// relationshipaddict.com/Obsessivelovewheel.html.

8. Neil Clark Warren, *Finding the Love of Your Life*, 93.

9. Gary Thomas, "Soul Mates or 'Sole' Mates?" www.focusonthefamily. com/marriage/preparing_for_marriage/searching_for_a_sole_mate/ soul_mates_or_sole_mates.aspx?p=1143782.

10. Rachel Cook, "Meaning in a Meaningless World," http:// rahablegacy.blogspot.com/2009/08/modern-day-rahab. html#comments

11. Michelle Skinner, "Listening," www.stfrancis.edu/content/ba/ ghkickul/stuwebs/btopics/works/listening.htm.

12. Caroline Leaf, *Who Switched Off My Brain?* (Nashville, Tenn.: Thomas Nelson, 2009), 46.

13. Dictionary.com. Dictionary.com Unabridged. Random House, Inc., http://dictionary.reference.com/browse/crisis.

14. Kim Clement, "Hope in the Midst of Chaos," hwww.elijahlist.com/ words/display_word/4256.

15. Caroline Leaf, *Who Switched Off My Brain?*, 15, 41.

16. Joanna Weaver, *Having a Mary Spirit* (Colorado Springs, Colo.: WaterBrook, 2006), 81

17. "Uncontested Divorce Information," www.alumbo.com/article/42413-Uncontested-Divorce-Information.html.

18. Lysa Terkeurst, "Affair Proof your Mind," http://lysaterkeurst.com/2011/01/affair-proof-your-mind/.

19. Caroline Leaf, *Who Switched Off My Brain?*, 65.

20. Henry T. Blackaby and Claude V. King, *Experiencing God* (Nashville, Tenn.: LifeWay Christian Resources, 1990), 87.

21. Don Raunikar, *Choosing God's Best* (Sisters, Ore.: Multnomah, 1998), 72.

22. Henry T. Blackaby and Claude V. King, *Experiencing God*, 56.

VISIT CHRISTYJOHNSON.ORG

Want more from Christy?

Head on over to www.ChristyJohnson.org
for tons of free resources, videos and
relationship wisdom.

You can also find out about Christy's
coaching programs or invite her to speak at
your next women's event.

Contact Christy at
Christy@ChristyJohnson.org.

CPSIA information can be obtained
at www.ICGtesting.com
Printed in the USA
LVHW022310090919
630430LV00021B/1447